Found

Advance Praise for
FOUND

A woman of great faith faces the most difficult situation anyone can face, including impending loss of life, and is saved by a miraculous intervention. Her life journey continues as she becomes a true force to help other victims and those in need…bad things equip believers for deeper ministry. Those with battle scars can better help those going through battles. Michelle Corrao's story is a compelling story of faith, courage, and resilience.

Neil Moore, ED.D., Fort Wayne
Chief of Police (ret.) FBI-LEEDA

Found is a powerful testimony by a courageous woman who has turned pain into power through an unimaginable ordeal. Michelle Corrao's story will encourage anyone who has been victimized, robbed of hope, and facing death. She is an incredible role model for survivors who are determined to not simply survive but go on to thrive through helping other survivors."
Casey Gwinn, President, Alliance for HOPE International

Through the eyes of a heroic survivor of kidnapping and brutal assault, *Found* is a gripping memoir that illustrates the harrowing story of the emotional and physical aftermath of sexual violence as well as the importance of a trauma-informed response. Vulnerable and brave, *Found* is an essential read for law enforcement, first responders, advocates and anyone who wants to be inspired by the resiliency of the human spirit.

Angela Rose, Founder PAVE: Promoting Awareness, Victim Empowerment, ShatteringThesilence.org

Found is a powerful story of indomitable spirit, faith, and service. It takes you on a terrifying yet inspiring journey that begins by challenging your belief in the intrinsic goodness of humankind and culminates with a true understanding of inconceivable perseverance and the power of hope. The book is a must-read for advocates, law enforcement, and others who work in or who want to work with sexual assault survivors. Michelle's heartbreaking and motivational story serves as an instructional guide to best understand a victim's tumultuous and painful, yet unique and often non-linear path to healing."

Laura Berry, MA Executive Director Indiana Coalition Against Domestic Violence

Found is a powerful and moving message of faith, hope and perseverance proving a window into God's love, grace and mercy for us. A lifeline for others offering hope, strength and courage. Truly a remarkable life story!

Beth Gehlhausen, Founder of Prevail, Executive Director Meals on Wheels, Hamilton County, IN

This is an incredibly important and powerful work, written from the mind and the heart of a true survivor who doggedly prevailed over her darkest night to live brighter and better days for herself and all those affected by such vicious and invasive crimes. *Found* is at once shocking, painful, inspirational and enlightening. It should be required reading for those who know and those who don't know. You will shed a tear and, eventually, smile broadly as you read Michelle Corrao's first-hand account of helplessness turning into determination, fueled by assistance, faith and heroism.

Steve Greenberg, co-founder and co-owner of
Current Publishing, and an 11-time author

Michelle revisits the painful suffering she's endured and uses it to give hope and encouragement to others. This is a story of triumph over tragedy, faith and recovery, love and fate. Reading her story will give you a refreshed look at the power of faith and human will and it breathes life into "I can do all things through Christ who strengthens me – Phil. 4:13"

Jennifer Wiese, Founder/CEO BeeFree LLC

Michelle's direct account of her courageous story of triumph over tragedy gives hope to victims and provides valuable insight to those who help them. A must read!

SFC Bethany Guzman, United States Army

Michelle gives victims of sexual assault hope and assurance that life following such a devastating tragedy is most definitely worth living and loving. This masterful book of faith and love reassures us all that the evil acts of others do NOT define who we are. Out of a horrifying night of terror and a resulting legacy of struggle blossoms a story of love and faith only Michelle can tell. Her vulnerability and strength make Michelle Corrao the perfect person to narrate a nightmare of evil, turned to triumph.

Judi Johnson, Director of Economic Development-CPM EcDMP 2012-2019

Michelle's story will engage you like no other story you have read. Reading *Found* is to live her terrifying and redemptive story. Although my heart broke and I cried as I read the horror and terror Michelle experienced, her undefeatable spirit lifted and inspired me beyond measure. This is a must-read for anyone who has faced a tragedy or great challenge in life. Truly an inspirational and unforgettable story.

Esther Lakes, Carmel, IN

FOUND

Triumph Over Fear
with Grace and Gratitude:

The Michelle Corrao Story

Michelle Corrao
with Emily Sutherland

NEW YORK

LONDON • NASHVILLE • MELBOURNE • VANCOUVER

Found

Triumph Over Fear With Grace and Gratitude: The Michelle Corrao Story

Published in New York, New York, by Morgan James Publishing. Morgan James is a trademark of Morgan James, LLC. www.MorganJamesPublishing.com

ISBN 9781631951480 paperback
ISBN 9781631951497 eBook
Library of Congress Control Number: 2020936687

Cover Design by:
Christopher Kirk
www.GFSstudio.com

Interior Design by:
Chris Treccani
www.3dogcreative.net

Morgan James is a proud partner of Habitat for Humanity Peninsula and Greater Williamsburg. Partners in building since 2006.

Get involved today! Visit
MorganJamesPublishing.com/giving-back

To Chris, Christian, Olivia, and Art.
Without you, my story would have
turned out very differently.
I love you.

Contents

Acknowledgments

The timeless poem "Bits & Pieces" has proven true in my life. I am a testament that everything life deals us can ultimately help us become the people we were always meant to be. The good and the bad, the pain and the healing, all have a way of creating a breathtaking mosaic that represents more than we could ever become alone.

People move in and out of each other's lives, and each leaves his mark on the other. You find you are made up of bits and pieces of all who have touched your life, and you are more because of it, and you would be less if they had not touched you.

The following people, and so many others, have created wonder and beauty in my life that I couldn't possibly have imagined. Without the following individuals, you would not be holding a redemptive story in your hands right now. First, all my thanks to God!

To the love of my life, Chris, thank you for believing in me and loving me always. Look at us now! I love you forever!

To the sunshine of my life, Christian Arthur and Olivia Kristine, thank you for teaching me a love like I have never known and more about life than I ever thought possible. I love better because of you. You are my heart! I love you more, most, best, always.

To my Mom Judy, whom everyone loves and who is my biggest cheerleader in life, and to Ross, thank you for always being there for me. I love you!

To my sister, Lisa, what would I do without you. Thank you for always being there for me and doing life with me. My brother-in-law, Tom, thank you for standing with us! To my nephew, Adam, I am so thankful that I'm here to watch your growth and say "I love you." To my niece, Rachel, her husband, Sam, my great-niece, Charlotte, and great nephew, Max thank you for being my inspiration and joy. You make me want to be a better person.

To the whole wonderful and fun Corrao family, thank you for your unending support, love, festa, and wedding celebrations. A special shout-out to the best father and mother-in-law, Andy and Marie, Salute! And Jim Zager, thank you for your inspiration and belief in me and this book. Cheers!

My hero, Art Billingsley, thank you for answering the voice of God and saving my life. We share a bond that is indescribable. What a blessing it is to celebrate life with you.

To my mentor and dear friend, Beth Gehlhausen, thank you for caring for victims of crime and abuse and doing something about it in founding Prevail, where victims are heard and seen every day. Thank you for allowing me to be part of it with you.

To the friends who are like family, both new and old, who have provided support, love, comic relief, and beautiful experiences that sustain me: Nate and Sara Hoeffel, Dave and Amy Gunderson, Bobby Hutner, Patty Leslie, Jeff Schlegel, Rich Burleson, Mr. Jacquay, Hiram and Marianne Rivera, Chuck and Nancy Flaugh, Jennifer Weise, Becky Richey, Wendy Boyer, Esther Lakes, Craig and Christi Crosser, Leslie Billingsley, John and Teri Ditslear, Roy and Judi Johnson, Kent Whitten, Ryan and Alisa Fisher, Dan and Patty Earle, Dr. Kristine Box, Julie Hoyt, Shannon Gigante, Ann Lemna, Becky Drews, Katie Pappas, Lee Calvin, Susan Tibbs, Kristen Boice, Dawn Crossman, Barb Patrick, Sandy Erghott, Carrie Renner, German and Maggie Holguin, Jennifer Blissett, Bonnie Rameriz, Lisa Heldman, Brian Kelly, Steve Greenberg, Jenni Backs, Father Christopher Shocklee, Dr. Susan Maisel, my Christ Renews His Parish teams, and my Riverview Retreat sisters. You have forever blessed my life.

To those individuals who have given me opportunities I couldn't have possibly dreamed of. You have honored me with your trust and friendship: Sue Carbon, Kristina Korobov, Karen Hensel, Barb Bachmeier, Angela Rose, Laura Berry, SFC Bethany Guzman, Col. Ross Waltemath, Leslie Cook, Michelle Ditton and Angela Kuntz. Thank you for your undeniable passion to serve.

To those who helped me fight then and now: Neil Moore, Pat Smallwood, Karen Richards, Sofia Rosales-

Scatena, Chris Meihls, Paul Shrowder, Jocelyn Butler, Sharon Langlotz, Mary Neddo, The Fort Wayne Sexual Assault Treatment Center, Casey Gwinn and Gael Strack and all first responders. Thank you for continuing the fight for others and never giving up. I am honored to call many of you friends.

"Victory is knowing you have fought for me no matter what the outcome is."

–Kristina Korobov, Assistant United States Attorney

To the incredible people at Prevail, the Prevail Speakers Bureau and The O'Connor House who have served with me to create healing and safety in our community and beyond, I am so grateful for you, for the work we have done together, and for the work we will continue to do for others.

Thank you to Brenda Alexander and Chris Colcord, who helped dig deep with me and kick start this book.

To Rebecca Hession and Jenni Robbins, thank you for inspiring me and literally cheering me on to make this happen.

From the bottom of my heart, thank you to Emily Sutherland for walking with me to write my story. You have a forever place in my heart.

Thank you to Morgan James Publishing for welcoming me into your family, embracing and believing in my story and finding it worthy to publish, I am honored!

To all the courageous heroes whose stories are similar in some way to mine, keep going!

I sincerely thank and love each of you. It is impossible to capture everyone whose presence has made an impact. I'm grateful to the many people in my life who have provided hope, healing, and friendship. You make the world a safer, more wonderful place.

Chapter One

Top Story

*A prerequisite to empathy is simply paying
attention to the person in pain.*
—Daniel Goleman

No one aspires to become the top story on the nightly news. The top story is reserved for tales of brutality, corruption, tragedy, or, on a good ratings night, a combination of all three.

On the evening of Friday, September 13, 1996, residents of Fort Wayne, Indiana were settled into their sofas and lounge chairs for the start of the WANE-TV 15 Alive News on channel 15. Co-anchors Karen Hensel and Lee Kelso looked into the camera somberly to report my attack on the nightly news. In measured tones, Kelso began relaying my story:

Our top story tonight: Women in Fort Wayne can rest a little easier now that the men thought to be responsible for as many as four sexual assaults are behind bars. The latest attack came late last night. A man allegedly abducted a woman from the 2400 block of South Wayne Street when she was walking to her apartment. According to reports, they hit her over the head and stuffed her into the trunk of her car. Police say they then brought her here to the 2900 block of Winter Street where she was sexually assaulted. Their last stop, this lot in the 7500 block of Kinnerk, is just south of Bandidos restaurant, and that is where News Channel 15's Mary Collins is right now to tell us about a series of events that unfolded last night there.

Throughout the viewing area, people were once more confronted with evil emerging in their community. Perhaps viewers shivered upon hearing of the fourth rape in the area. But, upon learning that authorities had identified three men in connection with all four attacks, it would be no surprise if the news brought as much relief as concern to locals—even more so if the attacks happened a comfortable distance from their homes and the places they frequented.

As the top story unfolded, images flashed across screens, revealing corner street signs and stately trees lining a sidewalk in partial disrepair along older, well-maintained homes and yards. Shockingly, anyone watching could see exactly where the latest victim lived.

Armed with this information, they would likely judge for themselves whether or not the victim made poor decisions. Had she chosen to live in a dangerous neighborhood? Was it a neighborhood they would live in or walk in? Would they be out at ten o'clock on a Thursday night? Would they park on the street?

Each *no* would make it easier for viewers to distance themselves from the violence and randomness of the attack. Each *no* took away their sense of personal alarm, allowing them to lower their raised eyebrows, settle more comfortably into their sofas, and perhaps briefly lament that such violence occurred in their hometown.

The news segment took only four and a half minutes. That's all the time necessary to lay bare the most intimate and terrifying moments of a life.

But not just any life—my life.

Viewers who followed the story over the next twenty-four hours would learn that I drove a shiny, new red Chevrolet Cavalier. They would see my personal items—clothes and bags—strewn across the backyard of my home and along the wooded area behind Bandidos.

They would learn I was sexually assaulted by three men and see what the crime scene looked like in the daylight. They would even see photos of one of the assailants, no doubt observing how very young he was and wondering how evil could look like a baby-faced nineteen-year-old.

Viewers would also learn that I was hit over the head and suffered lacerations, that I was stuffed into the trunk of my own car. Yet all of this horror—this voyeuristic trip away from the viewers' sense of safety—was quickly buffered as reporter Mary Collins continued, live from the

Bandidos parking lot: "That's right, Lee and Karen. It was a true nightmare for one woman, but . . . ."

But. That single word, nestled into the middle of a news update, took the story in a new direction as Collins continued her report, one that guided viewers' attention away from the horror of my worst nightmare in favor of a more a palatable message that focused on the hero who rescued me:

Fortunately, a member of the Fort Wayne Police Department was in the right place at the right time . . . . You see, after the suspects parked in the south lot, two of the men walked here to the back door of this Bandidos restaurant. That's where, fortunately, Detective Arthur Billingsley just happened to be searching this area. He saw the two men, scared them off, and they fled the scene. They ran back to the car parked in that south lot. Detective Billingsley happened upon the car but didn't know anyone was in it. As he began approaching the car, the men fled the car. He caught up with one of those men. That man, a nineteen-year-old suspect. As he was putting that man into [his] car, he heard a noise coming from the victim's red car. That's when he realized someone was in the trunk, and he rescued the victim. Now members of the Fort Wayne Police Department are calling Detective Billingsley a hero tonight. He says, however, he was just doing his job.

The community would certainly feel relieved that real heroes like Arthur Billingsley still exist and that the four recent acts of brutality to local women all pointed to the same group of men. If a single group of criminals was responsible, surely the world was not quite as dangerous as they originally feared.

This top story had already accomplished a lot. It revealed that a series of violent crimes in the community had been solved and produced a hero—albeit a humble one. What the top story could not accomplish, however, was any degree of healing for the ones whose lives were forever altered as a result of such brutality.

The course of my life was forever changed on that September night. That reality could not even begin to be communicated in a four-minute news story.

As the coverage continued, the image of reporter Mary Collins standing in the Bandidos parking lot gave way to footage of Detective Billingsley, who was dressed in a brown suit. His soft, hesitant voice redirected viewers from thoughts of his heroism to the suffering of the victim:

It's just kind of hard for me, personally, to feel like there was any heroism when she suffered lacerations to the head; plus, she was sexually assaulted. You know, it's kind of hard to feel like a hero when someone has gone through so much like that. Like I say, I think I could really have felt like a hero if I could have gotten to her before all that happened.

When Detective Billingsley opened the trunk of my car that night, he saw firsthand the terror in my eyes and saw a glimpse into what sexual assault by three men does to someone. He became the face of hope and humanity for me after a night of inhumane brutality.

To the media, however, I was seemingly the least important factor in the news report—dismissed as quickly as the facts became known that I was alive and had been reunited with my friends and family. What I would learn is that healing for victims doesn't come publicly and will never be resolved as easily as press reports convey. It is a long, personal journey that has barely begun by the time the media moves on to the next top story.

After reassuring viewers with thoughts of heroes who catch criminals, the reporter had to throw a bucket of ice water on the heroic narrative being communicated. Undaunted, Mary Collins once again appeared live from the parking lot of the Bandidos restaurant: "Fortunately, Detective Billingsley did get out here last night before a life was lost. And since that time, members of the Fort Wayne Police Department have been searching for the two suspects that got away."

Yes, all three suspects had been identified in the crimes, but only one had been apprehended. The previous report easing the community's fears was premature. And, also contrary to news reports, a life *was* lost that night. The loss of a confident, happy, secure woman was never recorded by a coroner, but that life was forever gone.

The woman whose timid thud on the trunk of her car—a trunk she had feared would become her coffin—was unrecognizable, even to me. Whether or not I would be capable of finding a new life remained to be seen.

The conclusion of that news segment, by reporter Deborah Cole, provided information about the three men involved in the attack. A nineteen-year-old, who had already been arrested and charged with criminal confinement and resisting law enforcement, had two previous convictions for carrying a handgun without a license.

The second suspect was twenty-three years old and faced more charges than the first—six to be exact—five of which were felonies that included aiding in rape and aiding an armed car-jacking. His criminal history included arrests for battery and criminal trespassing.

The last suspect was a twenty-one-year-old, who faced the same six charges and whose criminal history included arrests for battery and shoplifting.

Deborah Cole warned the public:

Remember, these three men are suspected in the four rape abduction cases in Fort Wayne this summer . . . . They battered some of their victims and used the victims' cars either to force the victims into the trunk or to make a getaway; they abducted the women near their homes and covered their victims' eyes . . . . Fort Wayne police are looking into another possible link, a similar event that happened this past Saturday in Bloomington.

With the summary of criminal history divulged, viewers might have had fleeting questions about how all three men with criminal histories were free to perpetrate such brutality on new victims. But behind the heroic cop, behind speculation about the suspects, behind any voyeuristic curiosity of where and when the attacks took place, thoughts of victims can quickly evaporate with one simple phrase, "In other news . . . ."

Chapter Two

My Story

*Our first responsibility in the midst of violence
is to prevent it from destroying us.*
—Henri Nouwen

The first sensation I felt when I regained consciousness in the trunk of my car was sheer terror. I could hear voices outside the car and hoped the commanding voice I didn't recognize was someone who would help me. I couldn't ignore the possibility that he could be another tormentor who would keep this nightmare going.

I was blindfolded and dazed. Mercifully, my body felt numb. My mind was cloudy yet racing as I drifted in and out of consciousness. I could not believe this was happening. I kept thinking I must be having a nightmare. If I could just wake up, I was sure this wouldn't be real.

The carpet beneath me was saturated with my own blood, and I had somehow managed to undo the binding that was used to tie my hands behind my back. I took a chance and tapped on the inside of the trunk with my foot.

Then I waited in the dark, wondering through my foggy state-of-mind what would happen next.

Detective Arthur Billingsley heard the small thud and realized I was in there. Though he had no key, he began to talk to me from outside the car. Then I heard him through the back seat, which folded down to allow him visual access to the trunk.

The musty mechanic's rag my attackers hastily tied over my face had slid down, and the dim glow of the dome light allowed me to see the face of the detective. When the trunk finally opened, Detective Billingsley found me curled up in a fetal position.

I emerged from the tomb of my car into a new reality, with blinding lights and medical professionals everywhere. Everyone was depending on me, from the police to the EMTs to the nurses, doctors, and eventually the prosecutors. These professionals, each armed with years of training, were uniquely qualified to deal with what happened to me. I, however, was not.

The police had a mandate to catch the bad guy. The emergency medical team had a mandate to fix my physical wounds. The sexual assault nurse examiner (SANE) had a mandate to gather as much physical evidence as possible to ensure the prosecutor could win a guilty verdict. The detectives had a mandate to get a statement from me that showed consistencies between my rape and the other attacks in hopes of compiling enough evidence to catch the criminals and, ultimately, keep them from ever doing this again.

All these professionals—some with training specifically designed to help them handle a sexual attack—were singularly focused on the one person who had no preparation for this turn of events. I was confused, injured, in shock, exhausted, and terrified in a way that can only be fully understood by someone who has endured such a nightmare.

The world around me was focused on punishing the perpetrators and preventing future crimes, but none of that could help me through the grueling hours and days that followed. Despite having family and friends in abundance, help did not come readily or easily.

Victims like me, I've learned, also have a mandate that comes in stark contrast to everything the first responders want and need. That mandate is simply to survive. At times, that was all I was able to do. But surviving is a far cry from healing and further still, from thriving.

Eventually, I would need to process the trauma in a way that would allow me to rediscover security, self-worth, independence, and determination. I would have to grieve the loss of who I once was and who I might have been in order to fully embrace this new person who was relearning how to live in the disorienting aftermath of the attack.

For a long time, my personality was completely swallowed up by the status of *victim*. Fear became a way of life that infiltrated my relationships, career, and well-being. I was afraid to go out and equally afraid to let anyone in.

I could not see then how my anguish could ever turn to joy, my numbness to love, rage to peace, restlessness to patience, hurt to kindness, self-pity to goodness, abandonment to faithfulness, terror to gentleness, or infant-like dependence to self-sufficiency.

I would have to differentiate myself from the *top story* and embrace *my story.* That process was a long, winding journey that prioritized my healing over sensational footage or the public's sense of comfort. It was filled with stops and starts, highs and lows.

I share my story for one reason: that others might understand what is possible. I understand feeling alone and helpless; I felt like I would never be happy or safe again. But feelings don't tell us the truth about the future.

I couldn't have predicted the horror I would face as a result of that attack, nor could I have predicted the beautiful life that was able to grow out of the ugliest circumstances imaginable.

Chapter Three

That Day

You never know what's around the corner.
—Duff McKagan

*A*live. That's how I would describe my state of mind when I woke up on Thursday, September 12, 1996. Just five days earlier, I'd finally moved to a new apartment after a few difficult years. I'd been living with my mom until I could get back on my feet after my first marriage ended painfully.

I had purchased a red Cavalier after my divorce was finalized a year earlier. I bought it all by myself, and that car represented more than transportation to me. It signified my independence.

On that Thursday, I was excited the weekend was coming and looked forward to getting home so I could get finish settling into my new apartment. I was happy to finally have my possessions out of storage so I could create a place that felt like home.

I worked for a construction management company, and one of our properties had a grand opening that evening in Michigan. Early in the morning, I picked up two of my coworkers at the company, and we made the three-hour trip north. It was a long, busy day, and the grand opening was a huge success.

That was before the days of cell phones to keep in contact with family and friends throughout the day. The long drive home that evening allowed my mind to wander to the good things in store for the coming weekend: a movie night with Chris, and a dinner we were planning with friends.

After work, I stopped by the grocery store to pick up ingredients and rented *Casablanca*, which was the movie we looked forward to watching as our Friday night feature. When I finally turned onto my street, the time was nearly ten o'clock. Still wearing the suit and heels I'd been wearing since early that morning, I was tired and eager to get inside.

My new residence was an older, well-maintained house, which had been divided into apartments. It was freshly painted in heather gray with bright, white trim and was situated in a row of similar houses on a slight hill. Residents parked on the street in front of the houses.

I started to park but noticed two men in dark, hooded clothing walking down the street. Something about their behavior made me uneasy. I obeyed the warnings of my intuition and drove around the block. When I got back around to the front of the house, they were gone.

As I parked, I noticed that neither my roommate's car nor the car that belonged to our upstairs neighbor was in sight. I wondered where the two men went but decided not to worry about it. I gathered up all my things, trying to take everything in one trip: a work bag, my purse, the grocery bags, the video, and a bag of clothes still in my car from a class I taught at the YMCA a few days earlier. I then retrieved a pair of glasses from the trunk. With all those things in tow, I headed toward the entrance of the house.

Entry involved unlocking a door on the left side of the porch, traversing a short hallway, then unlocking an inside door to enter the apartment. The moment I stepped up to the first door on the porch and moved the key toward the lock, my real-life nightmare began.

Chapter Four

Abducted

Something unexpected sent me plummeting to the ground.

A wave of terror washed over me as I suddenly realized I had been struck on the head with something hard.

Is this really happening?

As my sluggish thoughts tried unsuccessfully to process what was happening, I heard a deep, eerily soft voice from behind and above me ask, "Got any money?"

I screamed. Then, as I filled my lungs to scream again, a handgun flashed in front of my face. The gun was in the hand of the man with the eerie voice, and he warned me, "Look at it. I will use this if you don't shut up. Where's your money?"

Money—he just wants money. I can do this. I can handle this. I just need to give him my money, and he'll go away.

Still on the ground, I handed him the bills from my wallet without looking up and uttered, "Take my purse, my car, whatever you want! Please, just leave me alone."

If I don't look at him, maybe he will go away. I won't be able to identify him, and he won't need to kill me.

He didn't leave.

"Pick up your purse and come with me. Act like nothing happened." I could feel the gun in my side and his arm around my shoulders.

"Don't look at me," the soft voice commanded.

He steered me to the backyard where two more men were waiting. Again, I found my body crashing to the ground as he shoved me to my knees. Facing the back of the house, he spoke to me while the other two tried to decide who would bring my car around.

"We need to use your car for something," he explained nonchalantly, as if this was a common occurrence.

"Please, just take my car. Leave me alone," I begged.

The car that previously signified a sense of freedom and accomplishment suddenly meant nothing to me.

His voice sharpened. "No way! Do you think I'm stupid? You'll go to the police."

He paused. Then he asked, "Who do you live with?"

The other two strangers were rifling through my purse while he held the gun at my head. They found a five-dollar bill loose in the bottom of my purse that I had forgotten to give them when I emptied my wallet.

"You b****!" one of them blurted out.

"Two people live here," I responded to the question.

"How old are they?" he asked.

I didn't answer.

"Are they home?"

"One of them is. I saw his Jeep out front," I lied. The Jeep parked out front did not belong to anyone living in my home, but I was grasping for any possible hope of deterring them from whatever they had in mind.

I started praying silently. Both of the other men were gone; then I heard the car approaching through the alley. They must have both gone together to get my car.

The man with the soft voice attempted to tie a piece of cloth around my mouth, but it didn't work because the cloth wasn't long enough. So he gave up and, instead, used it to tie my hands behind my back.

He pulled me to a standing position, stuck the gun in my back, and ordered me to look down.

"If you cooperate, we won't hurt you." He then led me toward the alley where the car was idling.

On the way to the car, I heard the voices of people walking and talking. As their voices seemed to get closer, the man holding my arm told me to be quiet and pushed me to the ground so they wouldn't suspect any trouble. Through the darkness, I couldn't tell for sure what was in front of me, perhaps shrubbery or small trees, that would keep me out of view.

To keep me from screaming for help, he pushed the gun harder into me without a word, as if to warn me. Then I could feel the barrel pressed into my skin as he ran it up and down my side, back, and neck. I froze. I believed he was nervous enough to pull the trigger.

I couldn't feel any physical pain, but my mind kept recording every detail of what was happening. I could see that one of the other two men also had a gun hanging from his hand.

The voices from down the alley continued, and my mind kept racing to find a way out. I wanted to get someone's attention, but I was willing to do whatever they told me to do in an attempt to save my life. Perhaps they sensed how badly I wanted to scream because one of them found another cloth to tie around my mouth to make sure I stayed quiet.

When the voices dwindled off, the men opened the trunk of my car and returned to the backyard. They demanded that I climb the fence that separated the backyard from the alley. My hands were still tied behind my back, and I was wearing the red suit I'd worn to the grand opening. There was no way I could climb the fence in the long, straight skirt and jacket.

"Take off your shoes," one of them ordered. When I did, they picked me up and threw me over the fence. And in that brief moment, I saw their faces for the first time.

These were the men who had been walking down the street in front of my apartment just a few moments earlier.

Did they follow me? How did they know I was coming home to an empty house?

My mind recorded detail after detail: the moderate sixty-degree temperature that evening, the musky smell of the men. But I felt completely detached from my body. Part of me knew what their intentions were, but I couldn't process it in any helpful or meaningful way.

Next they tossed my belongings from the trunk onto the ground and shoved me into the cramped space. Raw panic roiled inside me, but I attempted to reason with them.

"Please don't put me in the trunk. I'll suffocate! Please, no!"

In my mind, I was screaming, but they barely seemed to hear my protest.

Alone in the trunk of my car, I was able to free my hands. Whenever the brake lights penetrated the thick darkness, I frantically searched for a way out. When the darkness returned, I clenched my hands in prayers of desperation.

Over and over, the brake lights went on, then off. I searched for a way out, then prayed when everything went dark.

I strained to hear what they were saying, hoping to make sense of their plans. Conflicting ideas raged in my head: a certainty that I was going to die, along with an overpowering fear of making any noise that would further agitate them.

I tried pushing and pulling on every raised piece of metal I could find in my blinded, cramped condition. I could never really see what I was doing, but my mind was working hard to help me survive.

At one point, I removed the ruby ring from my finger—an heirloom from my maternal grandmother—and took off the bracelet I was wearing, which Chris had given me. I hid them in the small crevice between the seat and the floor of the trunk, hoping Chris, my mom, my sister Lisa, or *someone* might find them and realize that I had been in this trunk.

I refused to let these men take my precious mementos. This seemed like the only thing I could control in the moment. It was the only act of defiance I could manage. They would not get my ring and bracelet.

I continued to try to make sense of their garbled voices so I could prepare myself for whatever was next. But there was no way I could have prepared for what would follow.

The car stopped. It was hard to tell how far we traveled, but I guessed five or ten miles.

I heard a voice say, "Is not home." I could only hear every few words, and I could somehow tell that the man with the soft voice was driving.

Then a voice from the back seat took my sense of terror to new heights. "I want to f*** her."

Oh, God, what am I going to do? I have to get away! Please, God, help me. This can't happen. This can't happen to me.

The trunk popped open, and the man with the soft voice—whom I had come to assume was the leader—saw that my hands were free. He was angry and spoke harshly to me, but I couldn't even hear what he was saying. My mind was racing.

I have to get away. I have to get away.

My body wasn't connected to my mind. My mind wasn't connected to my senses. My thoughts were random, skittering.

Before I knew it, I was out of the trunk, and I could feel my hands being tied together, tighter and tighter, behind my back with what felt like a belt.

A dog barked. *Could that be helpful? Could the dog barking be a way to freedom?*

We were some place outdoors, but I couldn't tell where. I could feel dirt and gravel under my bare feet. I saw a Halloween mask sitting on the car before they wrapped a cloth around my face so I couldn't see. I heard the trunk slam shut.

A Halloween mask?

I could think of no way out of this nightmare. The leader shoved the gun in my side once again, forcing me to run while he gripped my arm. The cloth blindfold smelled like a car engine.

He forced me to run faster and faster, with bare feet, on a surface that seemed too rough to be pavement but wasn't dirt. I was struggling to keep running, and the long skirt only made it more difficult.

We approached a building, and I was forced to step up then duck my head to enter. I could feel the cold cement walls close around me, but they provided no protection.

It was in this barren building that my clothes were torn off and they took turns raping and sodomizing me. I could smell alcohol on their breath, even when they were behind me, and when they finally stopped, one of them approached my limp body and looked at my fingers, gently stroking my hand. Then he touched my leg timidly, as if I were fragile. His fake tenderness felt like a mockery.

"Hasn't your boyfriend ever done this?"

I cringed and gagged, again and again, certain I would vomit. I felt as if there was no physical or mental strength left in me. The pain was unbearable, and I could smell the blood from my head wound. One of the men mentioned the smell of it, too.

I begged the leader with the soft voice to let me go.

"Not yet. We need to use your car," he claimed.

"Please, please put my clothes on," I begged. I expected them to refuse, but one of them complied.

The buttons on my jacket had popped off when they tore it from my body, but at least it partially covered me.

"I've cooperated. Please, let me go," I begged.

"You have been cooperative, but I can't let you go," he said.

He grabbed my arm and led me out of the building. He then forced me to run again, pushing me ahead. I could once again feel the hard gravel and dirt with sore, bare feet as he pushed me ahead. My eyes were still covered. I couldn't see where I was going, and I was beyond exhausted. I felt too weak to take another step, but he forced me to keep running, faster and faster.

What will happen to me?

Judging from the feel of the surface beneath my feet, I assumed we were headed back to the car. I wanted this nightmare to be over, but I had no idea how it would end.

Hearing voices not far from us, the leader shoved me onto my knees behind some shrubbery to hide from whomever we heard talking. I didn't know where the other two men went, but the leader kept talking to me.

His voice was faint, and I had to ask him to repeat what he said. "Sorry. We had to stop, and those guys got horny, and you are pretty. Your kind doesn't even notice someone like me walking down the street. Do you have a boyfriend?"

How could he expect me to carry on this conversation with him? What does he want? How am I supposed to respond? He has a gun in my side. He's going to kill me. What else are they going to do?

The questions raced through my head too fast to guess at answers. This strange conversation he was trying to carry on with me was beyond surreal, but I didn't want to antagonize him. So I tried to answer. Could whatever I say next buy my life? My freedom?

"Please, let me go," I begged.

"Do you think I'm stupid?" he retorted.

"How long do you need my car? Just take it and leave me here."

Nothing.

Then the trunk opened once again, and the voices stopped. That's when they picked me up and shoved me back into the trunk of my car. At that moment, I was convinced I would die there.

They tried to start the car, but it wouldn't start.

"Hey, what do we do? The car won't start!", someone demanded.

They eventually figured out that it was in gear, and they got it started. They backed out fast, and I heard the tires squeal as they surged forward. They blared the radio, which drowned out everything they said and would keep anyone passing by from hearing me if I screamed.

A year earlier, when I drove that shiny red car off the lot, I never could have imagined the circumstances that would culminate to form my last ride in it. I freed my hands again. It was harder that time, but I was not giving up. I resumed searching frantically for a way out, but my strength was waning, and I was struggling to stay alert.

By the time they finally stopped the car and turned down the radio, I was only partly conscious. I tried to keep myself from passing out so I could listen to their conversation.

The man sitting in the back seat asked, "Should I stay with the car while you two go?"

What are they doing? Are they robbing someone? Is this a drug deal?

Then I lost consciousness.

Chapter Five

Rescued

Freedom is the open window through which pours the sunlight of the human spirit and human dignity.
—Herbert Hoover

I don't know how much time passed before I regained consciousness, but from inside the trunk, I realized there was a voice outside speaking firmly: "I don't care if you have a gun."

Then I heard something that sounded like a radio or walkie talkie. I was disoriented and trying to make sense of what was happening outside the car.

Could it be the police? Or is it some sort of drug deal?

I've never experienced such terrifying darkness.

I heard the same voice again and decided to take a chance. I tapped lightly on the inside of the trunk with my foot and held my breath. If the voices I heard were the men who put me in that trunk, they were going to be furious.

"Is someone in there?" the voice inquired. The person speaking definitely wasn't the voice of any of the men who had brutalized me.

"Please, help me."

"I am Detective Billingsley of the Fort Wayne Police Department. Hold on, and I will get you out."

***

September 12, 1996 had been a draining day for Detective Arthur Billingsley. He worked the second shift from three o'clock to eleven and had spent most of the night at a Fort Wayne hospital investigating a case of child abuse. Normally at the end of a shift, he would go back to the police station and fill out paperwork, but he was especially tired on this particular evening and headed straight home.

Arthur's usual habit was to drive through the area surrounding his neighborhood before going home. He would check on various businesses after his shift ended since eleven o'clock was closing time for several of the area restaurants and prime time for robberies.

"I was single, and I couldn't cook, so I knew what time the nearby restaurants closed," Billingsley clarified.

But this time, he pulled directly into the parking lot of his apartment building and turned off the engine to his unmarked police vehicle. What happened next, he can only attribute to the voice of God. He has no other explanation.

"I can definitely say, that night, I was told to go back out," Billingsley explained when asked how he ended up behind the South Bandidos restaurant around eleven-thirty that Thursday night.

"I was sitting in my car, the engine off, and I very clearly heard, 'No, Art, you can do it. You can drive around a little bit.' Instead of me praying for God to do this or do that, it was God telling me to start the car up, turn right, and go to Bandidos."

So he turned the engine over and headed out of his apartment parking lot. Once at the parking lot exit, Art had to choose to go left or right. Left would take him past several restaurants, and right would take him past Dairy Queen—which was closed for the season—and directly to the South Bandidos restaurant.

Arthur chose to turn right, heading straight for the very place where my abductors had just arrived. At that moment, from the trunk of the car, I was praying for a miracle. I was begging God to let me see my family again, pleading for a way out.

In and out of consciousness, I stayed alert long enough to learn that two of the men who had abducted me would be leaving the car, and the third was going to stay in the back seat to prevent me from getting away. My Cavalier had fold-down rear seat access to the trunk, which might have allowed me to escape. I didn't know what their plans were: were they robbing some place or getting drugs or just stopping at another location so they could rape me again?

Anything was possible, so I knew I should remain alert. I tried with all my strength to keep from losing consciousness until staying awake became impossible. My body finally gave in to the exhaustion, loss of blood, and the physical and emotional trauma. I passed out.

In that moment, Detective Billingsley was pulling into the back parking lot of Bandidos, which was owned by a friend of his. He saw two men standing by the rear door of the restaurant.

"My first impression was that they were restaurant employees," he recalled.

"Even though I'm a cop, it's just not part of my nature to be suspicious of people. My car was unmarked, and I wanted to make them feel comfortable, so I made sure they were able to see my police lights. I didn't want them to think *I* might be robbing *them*."

Instead of being comforted by the presence of a police officer, the two men took off running down a side street, which was adjacent to a wooded area. Their behavior forced Arthur to believe they must be suspects—suspects of *what*, he did not know.

He pursued them down a side street with his police radio in hand. He just wanted to talk, but before he got the chance to ask them anything, they had disappeared into a nearby wooded area. Then he spotted the red Cavalier parked adjacent to the wooded area and approached the car.

"I reached for my flashlight to investigate. Just as I was getting ready to run the license plate number, the car door opened up, and a third man took off running."

With his flashlight and radio still in his hands, he pursued the suspect and caught up with him.

"At that particular moment, my first order of business was to latch on to one of them. I caught him and brought him back to the car. Then, when I was getting ready to call it in, I heard a thump coming from the trunk. I couldn't believe what I was hearing."

His police training had prepared him to investigate a crime scene after the fact, not to rescue the victim of a crime-in-progress. Unusual as this scenario was, he had to rely on his instincts.

"Usually, we are called after the fact, and we take statements and then go from there. But this was different."

When he first heard the thump coming from the trunk, Billingsley had not yet secured the suspect. So, before going to the trunk, he placed the suspect on his stomach and handcuffed him while trying to piece the facts together in his mind.

He knew there were at least two other suspects nearby on foot, not in custody. He still hadn't had a chance to call for backup. But he did know that if he was trapped inside a trunk, he would want to hear the voice of someone safe.

"Is someone in there?"

"Please, help me," I managed to reply.

Shocked into a renewed sense of urgency, Arthur identified himself and said, "Hold on, and I will get you out."

"It was all so quick. It was a big shock," he recalls. "I mean—what is this lady doing in this trunk? What kind of animals do I have here? I told her not to worry and I'd get her out. I still had to secure the area.

"As far as I knew, I had two more guys out there who were getting ready to rob Bandidos. I didn't know if they were coming back, whether or not they had guns, and the detective car I was driving didn't have a cage."

Police officers use codes to call for assistance, including a code for back-up, a code requesting lights and sirens, and a code that calls every law enforcement person, from railroad police to university police, to show up.

Billingsley called in more than one of those codes, plus a signal that indicated a kidnapping, and brought in every officer on the south side of Fort Wayne, as well as a medical team.

"I didn't know what had happened . . . but I knew I needed medics."

In the three minutes that passed before rescue vehicles and first responders arrived, I was able to tell Arthur how to get the back seat down until he was able to secure the keys.

"I remember reaching out and touching her hands through the back seat," the officer reflected, adding, "I remember making eye contact with her, and my heart just sank. My mind was in total shock."

When law enforcement officers are dispatched to a scene, they typically know what to expect. But this was no ordinary crime scene.

"You don't just go walking into a crime in progress. That's what made this so shocking," Billingsley reflects.

I could tell he was shocked—maybe even more shocked than I was at that point. I could see sadness in his expression. I remember being flooded with emotions— fear, sadness, and terror—but when I locked eyes with him, I felt a much-needed rush of hope. Reality forced Officer Billingsley to focus again on the handcuffed suspect and the others who got away, but I will never forget that brief moment when my humanity and dignity were acknowledged with so much compassion.

Billingsley's efforts to pull out the back seat and my best attempt at kicking the seat from inside the trunk were not successful. I had to wait in the trunk a few more minutes and began to cry and shake. Maybe three minutes passed from the time Billingsley radioed for assistance until the moment when officers, medics, and other first-responders arrived.

I didn't want Billingsley to leave, but he needed to refocus his efforts on informing and equipping the arriving officers to apprehend the two suspects who were at large and take the one in handcuffs into custody. That's when a female officer named Sofia Rosales-Scatena introduced herself to me. She was a compassionate, welcome presence that brought great comfort in that moment.

However, even the presence of a female officer was daunting. I didn't want a single other person knowing what had just happened to me. Still, Officer Rosales-Scatena didn't tell me what to do. She allowed me to feel in control, which was truly helpful in those vulnerable moments. Although I'm sure she was doing what she had been trained to do, I felt genuine empathy from her. I felt empowered to ask for whatever I needed, if only for a moment of quiet without having to answer all the questions in the midst of the chaos happening around me.

Every minute seemed like an hour before the trunk actually opened, but as soon as the medical team opened the trunk and got me out, I asked them to call Chris. People were swarming around me, and lights from all the emergency vehicles lit up the night air.

I didn't realize how many people had arrived while I was still entombed in the trunk. I was mortified to look around and see an officer I recognized. I had graduated from high school with his brother.

While some of the memories of those moments are crystal clear, others I can't remember at all. I can't remember if I walked from the trunk to the ambulance or if I was transported by stretcher or carried. I don't know when they covered me with a sheet as my clothes were barely draped over me. I had suddenly gone from sensory deprivation to chaos and bright lights, so my biggest concern was getting to some place safe.

Once in the ambulance, the realities of my physical condition began to set in. I felt terrible. There were two medics examining my head wound. I couldn't even feel the head injury at that point, and I was confused. Tears rolled down my face as one of the EMS workers known as "Peach" kept me talking.

Meanwhile, Detective Billingsley transferred the handcuffed suspect into a squad car and drove his car back to work where he was still trying to sort out what happened when the eight o'clock shift arrived Friday morning.

At some point in the wee hours of Friday, September 13th, Detective Billingsley interviewed the suspect and took his statement. The local news had already started reporting on the events of the previous night—the hero cop, the rescued victim—and they requested an interview with the exhausted detective. With permission from the chief, he avoided the reporters, slipped out the door, and went home.

He later said, "I didn't avoid the interview because I needed sleep. I just wanted to get away. I was tired of hearing, 'Good job,' and 'You are definitely a hero.' Making eye contact with the victim made me feel like if I had been there and been able to stop this before she was hit on the head—then I might have felt like a hero."

It was noon on Friday when Billingsley finally crawled into his bed, but before going home to sleep, he received word that one of the two suspects at large had been taken into custody and was being interviewed by another detective.

Detective Billingsley had been on the Fort Wayne police force only two years when he discovered and rescued me that night. I am convinced God prompted Arthur Billingsley to be at the right place at the right time to save my life. He was the answer to my desperate prayers in the back of the trunk, and he refused to give in to his exhaustion to go find me. It was a miracle for which I am forever grateful. I can't explain it any other way.

Chapter Six

Processed

Never underestimate the valuable and important
difference you make in every life you touch,
for the impact you make today has a powerful
rippling effect on every tomorrow.
—Leon Brown

S everal detectives came rushing in and questioned me after I arrived at the hospital. I barely remember what they asked, only that I was sitting up wrapped in a sheet and answering their questions as well as possible in that state. I could feel their urgency because they knew two out of three of the men who did this to me were still on the run.

In the triage room, I seemed to be the only one who didn't know what to do. Unlike law enforcement and the

Sexual Assault Nurse Examiner (SANE), I had no training, no experience, no protocol to follow. The person in the room who was most traumatized, physically exhausted, and mentally drained was the one with all the answers, but I was in no way prepared to deal with all the questions.

After answering the nurse's basic questions, I was taken to the Fort Wayne Sexual Assault Treatment Center (FWSATC) to be "processed." I had no idea what they were talking about but soon learned that a SANE would be completing a rape kit to preserve evidence on my body in hopes of proving and serving justice to the criminals who did this. I would also learn that there are extensive protocols followed to test for diseases and other potential complications.

I couldn't have possibly prepared myself for that experience. My body was a crime scene unto itself. Cameras flashed in my bloodshot eyes as photographs were taken of my uncovered body. All parts of my brutalized body were swabbed to collect samples. The SANE feverishly, yet painstakingly, recorded every bruise and tear.

I had eaten dirt at some point, yet I couldn't take a drink of water or brush my teeth. I was not even allowed to rinse out the taste of mechanic grease from the rag they tied around my mouth. At one point, I was fingerprinted and never told why. I felt as if my battered body wasn't mine at all. It had become evidence.

I had never been victimized before and suddenly longed for some semblance of dignity and perhaps a warning about what to expect next. I kept stating that I wanted to "wash this off"—not just the blood and dirt but the entire experience. I felt filthy and out of control. All I could think about was taking a shower, putting on clean clothes, and feeling more presentable. I was bothered when police and medical professionals came into the room to talk to me while I looked like that.

I wasn't accustomed to going anywhere without showering or fixing my hair and make-up. Even on weekends or when I worked in the yard, I didn't want anyone to see me disheveled and unclean. I wanted so badly to somehow to regain my sense of dignity.

How can they take me seriously looking like this? I wondered. *If I can't talk to the police confidently, how can they see me as a reliable, competent witness?*

I felt agitated throughout the examination, perhaps because of my confusion and shock but also because I did not have any information about what this process would entail or what would happen next. I looked to the SANE to help me understand what to expect, but I got the sense that she was not confident about how to communicate with me or put me at ease. No doubt it would have been unpleasant for her to tell me what she was going to do, and I'm sure interacting with me was not easy due to my traumatized condition. When she took a phone call during my examination while I waited, I felt as if she didn't really understand or care how I felt during such an invasive and excruciating process.

Every minute that I couldn't shower felt like an hour. I kept asking if the examination was almost over. The process seemed to drag on and on. I didn't understand at that time what an immense responsibility it was for the SANE to collect every trace of evidence on my body. I just knew I couldn't stand how I felt and wanted it to be over so I could clean up. I wanted to feel like myself again.

I don't remember whether or not I was asked if I would like an advocate in the room with me. If anyone did ask me, I wouldn't have known why I would need one. Had I better understood the role of a victim advocate, I would have paid more attention. I just knew I didn't want anyone else to know what had happened to me, and I didn't want anyone to call my mom because of the pain all of this would cause her. In retrospect, maybe nothing would have helped me feel more comfortable, but I do know my ability to advocate for myself was simply nonexistent. I was too stunned and felt too powerless.

By the time the rape kit was finally complete, I had been lying on the examination table for nearly two hours with my legs in stirrups, as if I was undergoing a PAP test. I had been admitted to the hospital at a quarter to midnight on Thursday, and it was—as best I could tell—close to six o'clock on Friday morning when the examination was finally complete. For almost seven hours, I had endured the prodding and questioning, the loss of control, and the seeming indifference to my humanity in order to collect all the needed evidence.

Chris and Richie, a very close friend, struggled over whether or not to call my mom while they waited in another room. Chris was solely concerned with my wishes. I had specifically told him, "Do not call anybody."

I had also begged Richie not to call her when I saw him. So he waited, but as time went on, he felt more and more strongly about letting my family know.

Although they didn't agree, Chris was glad to have Richie's company throughout the long, tedious night.

"I think Richie added some semblance of perspective," Chris later reflected. "I was solely focused on Michelle's wishes."

Richie decided to contact my sister, Lisa, first. In the meantime, Chris was distracted by a constant monologue running through his mind that looped over and over again: *What is happening? This couldn't have really happened. This sort of thing happens on television but not in my life. Yet here I am in the hospital, and it's happening.*

The blood on his shirt was a sobering reminder that this was, in fact, real. What the attack might mean for our relationship never crossed his mind.

Once the painful and embarrassing rape kit was finally complete, I was given medicine to prevent potential sexually transmitted diseases; an antibiotic to prevent infection; a stool softener, because I was still bleeding from my injuries; and all kinds of information and instructions. It was all coming at me faster than I could take it in. I was asked to sign forms and listen to a long rundown of potential illnesses and complications to watch for until, suddenly, I couldn't process any more information. I shut down.

I was no longer hearing anything the medical staff was saying. I asked them to call Chris in so he could hear whatever they needed me to know. I was embarrassed. I was trying so hard to cooperate, but I couldn't take it anymore. The trauma, exhaustion, and sensory overload had taken me to my limit.

Chris took note of the nurse's instructions about each medicine and heard about each injury, including the mandatory AIDS test and when the results would come back. While I knew there was no doubt in his mind about the sexual assault, we didn't talk about it any further at the time.

Finally, I was permitted to take a shower around seven o'clock. Then, around eight on Friday morning, I was released from the hospital. Part of me was relieved to finally have some quiet and privacy, but I had no idea what to do next or where to go from there.

Chapter Seven

Chris

To love someone deeply gives you strength.
Being loved by someone deeply gives you courage.
—Source Unknown

Tall and handsome, Chris's demeanor oozes stability and approachability. He is reasonable and deliberate in everything he does. Long before we met, he had his life all planned out. He would get a job after college, get married, have three kids, and live a white-picket-fence kind of life.

He entered his first marriage with that characteristic diligence and intended to make it last forever. However, even his best attempts could not keep his first marriage together. His wife decided to end the marriage, and he felt like a failure.

My divorce had become final a year before I met Chris at a work-related golf outing, but his marriage had fallen apart only a few weeks earlier. Neither of us wanted to fall in love anytime soon. I was attracted to him, and he later admitted he couldn't stop thinking about me after we met. But we weren't ready to trust anyone or commit to a new relationship.

It was a few months after that first meeting when we saw each other again. He knew where I worked because my company had been a sponsor for the golf outing. But he resisted the urge to make contact for a while. One day our paths crossed outside my office building when he dropped by my company for a reason he later admitted he made up just so he could possibly see me and talk to me again.

We ran into one another a few more times, stopping to talk briefly in passing. During one such conversation, he learned that I was planning to attend a Notre Dame football game the following weekend. As fate would have it, he had tickets to the same game. He asked where I would be seated, and, to my surprise, he found my seat during the game and stopped by to say hello.

Certain that I would be worried that he was stalking me, he invited me and my neighbor, Sheila, who had invited me to the game, to meet up after the game, along with some friends he was sitting with. We took him up on the invitation, and he and I had a chance to talk at more length.

I still had no interest in a relationship. I was fine with being alone for the time being. I could think up all kinds of reasons I didn't want to date Chris: he needed more time to get over his divorce; I wasn't in the right place in my life for a relationship; he was too eager; I had too much baggage.

He really loved his ex-wife. We both needed to know that he had done everything possible to make it work. I never wanted either of us to feel like we were settling for "second best."

In spite of all my reasons for not wanting to date him, I eventually ran out of excuses and agreed to go have a drink with him. For a long time, our relationship consisted largely of long talks. I did most of the listening. His life crisis was fresh, and I was more comfortable listening than talking about my life. Besides, I needed to get to know him and learn all I could about him before trusting him with my own story. Countless hours of friendship, many long talks, and a great deal of patience on Chris's part slowly built a foundation of trust. What we had gradually grew from friendship to romance.

On the night of September 12, 1996, with Chris's ex-wife firmly in his past, we felt hopeful about the future, but we were making no plans for marriage. We just knew we wanted to be in each other's lives. Up until that time, though, he only knew the version of me I had allowed him to see.

On that fateful evening, he knew I was going to have a long day and didn't expect me to return from Michigan until late. So he was not concerned that he hadn't heard from me yet. When his phone rang around ten-thirty, he expected to hear my voice and answered with a smile.

Instead of my voice, however, he heard the voice of my friend, Richie, who was an Indiana State Trooper.

"Chris, are you with Michelle?"

"No, why?" Chris responded, trying to process why Richie would be calling with this question.

"Well, I'm at her place, and her car is gone, and some things are here, and there's blood all over."

"What are you talking about? What do you mean?" Chris's tone turned to bewilderment as his mind tried to make sense of what he was hearing.

"Well, her stuff is here on the ground, and there's blood."

Chris vaguely remembers telling Richie he'd be right there before hanging up the phone. He lived on the north side of town, but he'd never made the trip faster than he did that night.

Chris had a bag cell phone at that time, but I did not. In those moments, there was no way he could call me, no way of finding out what happened.

While making his way across town as fast as possible, his mind searched for a reasonable explanation. *Maybe she fell and hit her head and her roommate took her to the hospital.*

There was no scenario that made sense. He knew something wasn't right.

When Chris pulled up in front of my home, there were police officers combing the property. Richie had friends on the Fort Wayne Police Department, and he had called them to the scene, trying to put the missing pieces together.

When Chris spotted Richie, he walked up to meet him on the front steps toward the entry door asking, "Do you know where she is? Have you heard anything?"

Then Chris spotted my billfold in the space between the two entry doors. There was blood on it and around it. My personal belongings were scattered about.

He still recalls the confusion he felt: "In my analytical nature, I was trying to make sense of what this really meant. Did something happen or not? I kept talking to Richie—we'd pace and talk, and he'd go talk to the police, and then we'd talk again. We were trying to put together her day and figure out her plans. I hadn't talked to her since the morning. Her car was gone, so we wondered if she had driven herself somewhere."

Richie called around to his fellow officers to find out if there had been an accident. After one call, Richie suddenly spoke up: "Chris—I think they found her. We have to go."

"What do you mean?"

"They found her. She's in an ambulance. They're taking her to the hospital."

At this point, Richie knew more than he was telling Chris. He drove his trooper car fast—emergency lights on—and Chris followed closely behind him. They covered the distance from my home to the hospital in no time.

When they arrived, they saw other police officers who had just arrived with the ambulance. Richie rushed to meet them.

"I need to get this guy to her!" he explained.

As Chris rushed into the emergency entrance of the hospital, he clearly remembers hearing me calling out his name. He followed my voice to the triage room where I was being treated. When he got there, Officer Sophia Rosales was still there with me, and he rushed to my side, seeing that I was bleeding but still having no idea what had happened.

"I think when I walked into the hospital, I somehow realized Michelle had been sexually assaulted, but I didn't know to what extent," he reflects. "I just remember the only thing I was thinking is that I have to hold her. And I did, for what seemed like forever."

He remembers the moment vividly: "I kind of sat and leaned over the bed. I hugged her and just held on to her."

I was disheveled and not cleaned up at all. I had blood in my hair and on my face. My clothes were sort of draped over me, and I was still in shock, staring blankly, unable to say much.

Chris recalls having a white shirt on, and when he hugged me, blood got on his shirt. He remembers me saying, "Oh—I'm getting your shirt all bloody," and all he could think was, *She's been through something awful, and she's all worried about my shirt?*

The next thing Chris remembers is me telling him my head hurt. He looked and saw a gash on my head that hadn't been treated. He asked if I had been x-rayed or if they had done anything about my head wound.

He was frustrated when I told him they hadn't done anything about it yet. That gave him something tangible to do for me, so he called over a nurse and told her I had been hit on the head and needed an X-ray or CAT scan. Chris accompanied me down the hall and sat just outside the room during the scan; then he returned with me to the examination room.

I don't remember the scan. I don't even remember the staples being put into my head. But I do remember the doctor returning to the triage room to inform us that my skull was not fractured and there was no bleeding inside my brain. Then he stepped out, and that's the last we saw of him.

He didn't acknowledge my trauma, perhaps for the sake of efficiency. Whether or not it was his intention, the cold interaction communicated to me that my trauma meant nothing to him. Not having my humanity acknowledged made me feel small, like my trauma was no big deal.

For the remainder of that night, time compressed and ran together. I was told that Rosales stayed with us, and Chris was able to answer some basic questions so I didn't have to. Chris remembers me leaning on him as they began the questioning.

"I don't think they even asked what happened," he later reflected. "Michelle was vacant from the moment I walked in. She knew it was me, but it seemed like there was nobody home. She was just staring blankly."

I did not have the energy to fight the process or to figure out what to do or say. I was using all my internal resources just to get through each moment. The goal I'd set in my mind after I was rescued from the trunk was simply to make it through the next thing I had to do. I couldn't even think about the future or what any of this might mean for Chris and me.

As Chris and I made our way toward the hospital exit, the doors slid open in front of us. I looked through the glass of the second set of doors opening before us, and I saw my mom, my sister, Lisa, and her husband, Tom, walking toward us.

I will never forget the expressions on their faces when they saw me: a strange mixture of relief that I was alive, sadness, disbelief, pain, and worry. We embraced and cried together there at the hospital entrance. I don't remember anything that was said, if any words were spoken at all. No words were needed. Our tears and hugs said it all.

My prayer from the pitch-black trunk of my car had been answered inexplicably. I had survived long enough to be reunited with Chris, my mom, and my sister.

Chapter Eight

The Aftermath

In every community, there is work to be done.
In every nation, there are wounds to heal.
In every heart, there is the power to do it.
—Marianne Williamson

During the drive home from the hospital, Chris remembers looking over at me in the passenger's seat and seeing only the shell of me. I was absent. Changed. Empty.

I remember staring out the window in silence, watching cars coming and going, and two things were running through my mind. First, I wondered what was happening in the lives of the people going by and felt empathy for others' pain as never before. And, second, I was desperate to know there was someone out there who had survived something like this who could give me a glimmer of hope that I could survive, too.

By the time we arrived at Chris's home, the city of Fort Wayne was awakening to news reports of a heroic police officer and a break in the case involving multiple abductions and sexual assaults in our area. I was the fifth woman to be attacked by the "Trunk Rapists," as the media named them, and each attack had grown more violent than the last.

Television news showed footage of my red Cavalier, the front of my apartment, and the street sign indicating the cross streets where the apartment was located. They reported that an arrest had been made. Thanks to Detective Billingsley, at least one of the three men was off the streets.

The Friday morning edition of the Fort Wayne paper, *News Sentinel,* disclosed still more details, including the location of the sexual assault and the address of the restaurant beside the lot where the first offender was apprehended. Although no one published my name, the reporter stated that "the victim" was treated at the Fort Wayne Sexual Assault Treatment Center at Parkview Memorial Hospital and later released. My privacy seemed to be a thing of the past as I watched the places and details of such personal trauma laid bare, even sensationalized, for the general public.

I didn't want to be known as "the victim," but I also had no idea what being a survivor would entail. I tried to drown out all the thoughts racing through my head long enough to rest, but I couldn't get my exhausted body to fall asleep.

I was most terrified about the possibility that the attackers might somehow track me down and try again to kill me. I stayed awake watching and listening for any signs of them. The sense of dread kept me from being able to breathe normally. I was in panic mode every moment.

Chris quickly realized that if I began to drift off to sleep then opened my eyes and couldn't see him, I would come unraveled. Even leaving me alone in the next room to get a drink of water would send me into panic mode.

There was nothing Chris could say or do that could keep me from everything I was feeling. But he stayed up with me and offered his calm presence. He was surely exhausted, too, after spending all night in the hospital with me, but he remained patient and calm.

Whenever I needed to use the restroom, I would ask him to stand outside the door. He patiently did whatever was needed, yet I was inconsolable. Nothing soothed my wracked nerves.

Tired yet wired, I was not coherent. Anxiety kept me from being able to function or concentrate on anything. I don't even remember eating. I normally had all my meals planned out ahead of time on any given day, but I didn't have the capacity to figure anything out, even what I wanted to eat.

Although I was totally dependent on Chris, I was simultaneously furious that he was doing everything for me. I felt lost, yet I wanted more than anything to appear normal and unchanged by what had happened. I resented the fact that the world was going on as usual when my world had been shattered by three people I'd never even laid eyes on twenty-four hours earlier.

Arthur Billingsley had quietly slipped out of police headquarters that morning to avoid reporters, at least temporarily. After getting some rest, he called Chris to check in and asked if he could stop by for a visit the next day. I was grateful for his thoughtfulness to come by and see how I was doing.

When he arrived, he wanted me to know right away that the media was portraying him as a hero and how uncomfortable he was with their depiction of him.

"I don't feel like a hero," he admitted.

He was a hero to me. He saved my life.

He went on to express how sorry he was about what happened and apologized that he didn't make it in time to prevent the attack altogether.

He updated us on what was happening with the two men who got away and said the police department was pursuing leads they hoped would enable them to locate the other two attackers.

Early the following week, two female detectives came by for some questioning. They didn't ask how I was doing or otherwise indicate that they cared about me at all. Their attention was entirely focused on the criminals, and the questions they asked were invasive and cold.

Looking back, I know they were just trying to do their jobs. But I already felt objectified, and the way they interacted with me heightened my disgust. I was under no obligation to be nice to them or provide the answers they were looking for. Then I felt guilty for not being more cooperative.

During the next couple days, I learned that I had been the final victim of the Trunk Rapists. The other two men were captured and turned on each other in an attempt to save themselves. Upon learning that all three were behind bars, I was surprised that I didn't feel relieved that they could no longer track me down. I remained worried that they could still get to me somehow. Yes, they were in prison, but my fear of them imprisoned me, too.

My family helped in every way they could. I never wanted to see my car again, so Lisa, kindly retrieved my grandmother's ruby ring and the bracelet from Chris that I'd hidden in the car.

Because the attack started at my apartment and the attackers knew where I lived, I couldn't think of ever returning there. A little more than a week after the attack, Mom organized family and friends to pack up the belongings in my apartment so I wouldn't have to go back. In short order, they moved me out of the apartment I'd lived in for only a few days.

Mom hosted a dinner for everyone who helped with the move, as well as for a few other friends and family members. She hoped the gathering would allow the people closest to me a chance to offer their support and wanted to create a place where they could gather around me rather than wonder whether or not to call, stop by, or engage with me about the attack.

The gathering was a little more than a week after the assault, so Chris and I were emotionally raw, not to mention frazzled from exhaustion, but we wanted to thank everyone for their help. Everyone was supportive, but nobody knew what to say. I didn't want sympathy. I couldn't stand being seen as fragile. Throughout the gathering, I felt like the elephant in the room. I heard people say how lucky I was—lucky to be alive. But I felt anything but lucky.

I couldn't stay for very long before I had to retreat upstairs. I was too overwhelmed to attempt conversations with people who couldn't possibly understand all I was dealing with internally.

What does it look like if I don't do what others expect of me? If I decide not to accept invitations to socialize, will I look weak? Will I look different from who I was?

I didn't feel comfortable being with people, and I didn't feel comfortable being alone. I tried support groups in an attempt to find someone I could relate to, but I didn't find anyone whose situation was similar to mine. Focusing on hating men or venting about the injustice of it all was not helpful or healing to me either.

I had plenty of people in my life who loved me and were willing to be there for me. But what I had experienced was, thankfully for them, beyond their frame of reference. I was lonely and had no idea how to cope.

At that time, I wasn't informed about post-traumatic stress. I didn't know how a traumatic life event like mine rewires the brain and nervous system, creating symptoms that cannot be controlled by sheer will. I thought I was going crazy. I longed to talk to someone who had been through something similar, but I had no idea where to look. If only I had known someone who could tell me that everything I was feeling was normal after surviving this kind of experience. It wasn't just the thoughts in my head that kept me frozen. The aftermath of this trauma took over my entire being: body, mind, and soul.

Every day was a first: the first Christmas after the attack, the first New Year's, the first birthday, the first summer. Between the PTSD and media coverage and trials, the reminders were constantly in my face.

In addition to the personal toll the attack took on me, there was a financial reality. My purse, identification, and credit cards all had to be replaced. My red suit was destroyed, along with the clothing I kept in the trunk for working out. I even lost the deposit and first month of rent at the apartment I only lived in for days.

Even filing an insurance claim for the losses was a difficult process. Adding insult to injury, the insurance agent asked me what I was wearing when I was attacked. Every question was a cruel reminder, and everywhere I turned presented another hurdle that I feared I couldn't jump.

My future, too, seemed to hinge on things I'd never had to worry about in my life. I had to consider the real possibility that the AIDS test would come back positive. Panic and uncertainty, including fear about the outcome of this monumental health threat, undermined my emotional and physical stability. It would take six months of AIDS tests, one each month, to lift this fear.

The only control I felt I could impose was over myself. So I locked myself inside Chris's home from dusk until dawn. In many ways, I felt like a prisoner. I would not leave the house after six o'clock. I couldn't be alone after dark. Every activity that I used to do without a second thought became a major hurdle. The tragedy was taking over my life.

I believed nobody could relate to what I was experiencing or the anxiety that coursed through my being every minute of the day. I wanted to know that someone could survive this. I wanted some thread of hope that a good, happy life was possible for me in the future.

Instead, more fear crept in. *What if I am being ridiculous and making too big a deal out of all this? What if I lose my job because I let this paralyze me?*

On September 30, a couple of weeks after my abduction, I started back to work. I was nervous to face people but was equally afraid that I would face criticism for not "getting over it" fast enough. Every day, even in broad daylight when I ventured out the door to work, there were moments when I became incapacitated because of unexpected sounds and smells that triggered panic. I became adept at hiding those feelings to keep up the charade that I was coping just fine. I choked down the overwhelming fear that came and went constantly. During those first weeks back at work, I forced myself to keep showing up and even tried to attend occasional social gatherings.

Mingled with the fear of losing my identity were intense feelings of resentment because other people didn't have to walk through life carrying this ball and chain of terror. No one could say or do anything that made me feel understood—not even Chris. I would say hurtful things to him, even when he was doing all he could to be sensitive to my complicated state of mind. I couldn't make sense of how I was feeling and didn't want to be treated like I was broken.

I started running again. Running had always brought me so much peace; it was my happy place. Yet it now came with fear. I resumed my work as a group fitness instructor, but my class dismissed at seven, which meant I had to rush home so the sun didn't set before I was safely locked inside Chris's house.

Each attempt at normalcy was accompanied by waves of panic that only made me feel like I was careening backwards instead of moving forward. When I tried to do things I had always enjoyed, I would frequently become filled with rage. It wasn't fair that I had to live in constant fear while everyone else just moved through normal daily activities without a second thought.

There were physical scars: the tracks left from the line of staples that ran beneath my hair; handprints bruised onto my legs, arms and thighs; the sleeplessness and resulting exhaustion; the pit in my stomach and muscle memory that caused me to recoil whenever I was outside, alone, or in a dimly lit area; the sensory triggers that threw me back to September 12, 1996, with no more than a whiff of mechanic's grease.

Most of my scars, however, were invisible to the eye. My own body repulsed me. I hadn't felt like it was my own since the attack. I found myself constantly avoiding mirrors so I didn't have to face myself. Besides, I hardly recognized the tired, haggard face staring back at me.

I tried to appear strong whenever I was around people, but in my heart, mind, and soul, a perfect storm was brewing. Every activity, behavior, attitude, or habit that was comfortable before the attack became a trigger. Even the personality traits that had defined me—trust, independence, fearlessness, and innocence—were altered. I felt unrecognizable in every way, and I didn't know where or how to find my way forward.

On October 5, less than a month after the attack, I took my first trip to run in a 5K work-related event in Dallas, Texas. I was afraid but wanted to prove I could run it and be around a lot of people. Chris came with me to Dallas, and we took a walk on a sunny afternoon. Of course, I would only walk in broad daylight. Everything was fine until we approached some shrubs. The mere sight of them caused my memory to flash back to the night I was forced to hide behind similar foliage with a gun pressed into my ribs.

Suddenly, without warning, all the terror I felt during the attack hit me like a tidal wave. Seemingly out of nowhere, I was brought to my knees by this unexpected reminder that willing myself to "get over it" was not going to happen as quickly or easily as I had hoped.

By some miracle, I was able to run the next day. But I would later learn that this kind of episode was a classic marker of post-traumatic stress disorder (PTSD), along with every other feeling I was experiencing in the aftermath of the attack: increased agitation, mistrust, anger, and the abrupt change in my normally-compliant, friendly demeanor. It was all simply my brain and nervous system trying to protect me from danger whenever reminders of vulnerability were triggered.

Many friends and acquaintances tried to connect with me, but there were very few I would actually talk to. I even struggled to know how to interact with my closest friends from childhood, who were still important parts of my life. I didn't know how to have relationships with anyone. I would not be able to reciprocate others' friendship for a while, especially the patience and kindness Chris extended to me during that time.

I didn't know it at the time, but trauma of any kind, particularly a violent attack, requires us to be kind and patient with ourselves. I felt totally isolated and unsure how life could ever feel "normal" again, but I was doing the best I could do, and that's all anyone can expect of herself.

Chapter Nine

Faith and Fear

*Faith is taking the first step even when
you don't see the whole staircase.*
—Martin Luther King Jr.

When you've experienced the brunt of evil, it's understandable for questions about God's goodness to surface. And perhaps it's natural to wonder where He is hiding when fear startles you awake in the middle of the night. But, for whatever reason, that was not my experience.

As I was curled up in the darkness of that trunk, staring death in the face, I felt that I was sharing space with a Loving Presence that was as real to me as a human being. In those moments, my desperate prayers were met with a peaceful awareness that I was not alone.

I have come to understand that shock is a way the human mind is wired to help us survive trauma. But there was something else going on, too. I was able to think, pray, and experience the holiest Presence I'd ever felt, even when my body was bleeding and my consciousness fading.

At one point, I could see my body from a different vantage point as if I were looking down on someone else's body. That was the closest to death I've ever been. Yet, surprisingly, in what should have been the worst moment of my life, I wasn't afraid to die. I knew God's Presence was with me, and it was more tangible than ever before.

I was so overwhelmed I wept. For the first time in my life, I could identify with Jesus' pain and suffering in ways I never could before. I wept over His suffering, yet also felt the keen awareness that He was weeping over mine, too.

I'd believed in Him since I was a little girl, and He was always a special part of my life. As far back as seven years of age, I started attending church with my neighbor's family and immediately felt like I couldn't get enough. There was something inexplicable that drew me in.

I could walk to the church located just behind our house, and I always felt at peace there. Since I no longer had a father figure at home, the idea of a heavenly Father was comforting. As I grew, I became more involved, and my sister and I sang for Saturday evening masses.

When I was a young teenager, my best friend, Sara, invited me to her church youth camp. That week away gave me a lot of alone time just to pray and worship, and it was the first time I ever remember taking the opportunity to sit alone and be quiet with God.

I came away from that camp experience with the awareness that God was taking care of me. My understanding of Him changed from believing that He existed to actually interacting with Him like I would a trusted friend. Camp taught me a kind of faith that went deeper than just formal prayers or reading the Bible, and I started communicating with Him. I began having conversations with Him and felt I could talk to Him about anything. For a heartsick little girl, this was an amazing revelation.

Looking back, I see those early faith experiences built a foundation that not only sustained me as a young girl who needed a faithful Father, but also prepared me for what was yet to come. He knew what I would need before I needed it.

I can't explain what motivated Arthur Billingsley to restart his car and drive through the neighborhood one more time. He couldn't have known what he would encounter when he listened to that inner prompting. But at the very moment he was about to call it a day, I was praying from the trunk of my car for God not to let my story end like that. I have no doubt God had a purpose left for me and intervened. There was no other reason for Arthur to restart his car after a long day. He listened and followed that instinct. And I am alive today because he did.

On the Saturday night following my abduction, I needed to feel safe. So Chris and I went to the one place where I had always felt safe and at peace. We went to church, and I took the opportunity to thank God for sparing my life and hearing my cries in the dark.

Clinging to God during the dark days that followed didn't make my fears or anger magically disappear. There was pain beyond description. The aftermath of the tragedy, with all the turmoil and mixed emotions, was more difficult than I could have imagined. But I had conversations with God about all that I was thinking and feeling, just as I had done when I was young. I knew I could be honest with Him.

I never thought I would make it through the physical and emotional trauma of that night, but God allowed me to live. I believe my answered prayer meant He still had plans for me.

I often questioned why God was putting all this heartache in my life. I begged Him to help me find relief from the fear and anxiety. But He did something even better.

Rather than removing my fear or making my life easier, He began making me stronger. Rather than taking away those awful memories, He showed me that I could survive even the worst experience imaginable. And rather than taking away my feelings of isolation, He put people in my life who patiently supported me and showed me kindness I might never have known had I not gotten so low.

I'm convinced God does not cause bad things to happen to us, but, in my experience, He did give me everything I needed to heal. That healing took time and diligence on my part. But I didn't have to do it alone. I know He brought Chris into my life at just the right time. Chris showed me God's love in human form, even when I could not reciprocate.

It is possible to hold fear and faith at the same time. And that is what I had to do to survive.

Chapter Ten

Steps toward Healing

I will love the light for it shows me the way,
yet I will endure the darkness because
it shows me the stars.
—Og Mandino

Fear ran my life for at least nine months following the attack. I was surprised and frustrated that I couldn't find my way back to any semblance of normalcy. As much as I wanted to will myself to move from "victim" to "survivor," I had no idea how to do that.

The truth is, going back would prove to be impossible. I could only move forward into a new normal. Life would always look different for me. That was a frustrating reality.

I started journaling as a way of trying to record all the thoughts and feelings that were spilling out of me. That proved to be a helpful place to process the pain, fear, and rage that were constantly tearing at my peace of mind.

My needs always seemed to conflict with one another. For instance, I needed respect and privacy while also needing the presence and comfort of people who wouldn't judge me. The confusion and pain that constantly seeped out of me was perpetually at odds with my fear of what people thought of me. I wanted to get through it, but I also felt incapacitated by it.

Now, in hindsight, I see that the healing began with a grieving process. I grieved all that was taken from me: the sense of safety I once felt, the confidence, the carefree outlook on life, the privacy, and the sense of control over my own well-being.

Grief is messy and hard, and I didn't feel that I was doing it very well. It certainly didn't feel the way I thought healing would feel. I'm not even sure what "grieving well" would look like. I had never had to do it before. Soon I learned that grief is such a mixed bag of painful feelings that are *normal* and *necessary* but *difficult*.

I didn't know to call it grief then, but looking back, I see all the classic stages: denial, anger, bargaining, depression, then eventually acceptance. These stages of grief didn't come in any particular order, and I moved back and forth between them all multiple times. When difficult emotions would surface, I often felt as if I were going backward in my healing instead of moving forward.

I grappled with the reality that my life had been upended in a matter of hours by complete strangers—

strangers who caused so much damage without a hint of remorse, not only to me but to other women as well. The injustice of that was maddening.

Denial showed up when I tried to appear unchanged. Stuffing all the emotions and faking my way through workdays and social engagements was my attempt at pretending the whole thing never happened. But denying it only resulted in exhaustion and exasperation. It didn't help me feel any better.

Inevitably, when I fooled others into thinking I was unchanged by the tragedy, I would hear things like, "You are so strong." Then anger would come. I'm sure that seemed like a good thing to say, but silence would have been better. Hearing people tell me I was strong somehow minimized this catastrophic event that took all the energy I had to survive. Even still, I didn't feel like a survivor any more than Detective Billingsley felt like a hero. Those comments made me feel misunderstood.

I needed to have the space to feel everything I was feeling. So there were a lot of people—even people I considered good friends—whom I couldn't bring with me into the difficult depths of the healing journey. Most of them couldn't understand what trauma had done to me. It took more energy than I had to try to tell them things I wasn't fully aware of myself.

The anger was especially hard for the ones closest to me. No one got the brunt of my anger more than Chris. I would tell him I just needed him to listen, but when he would do that, I became furious because he wasn't saying anything. He was only doing what I asked, but, wisely, he refrained from pointing that out. Chris was incredibly understanding, but I couldn't expect him to be everything I needed.

He says he was just doing the right thing because he loved me. But I know I made it very difficult most days. I can now acknowledge that I probably made it difficult for him to love me on purpose—to make sure he was really someone who wouldn't run away when things got hard.

I wanted so much to talk to someone who specialized in healing after sexual assault, but I couldn't find anyone with that kind of training or experience. A few years earlier, during my divorce, a friend I worked with gave me the phone number of a therapist named Jocelyn who helped me navigate the difficult end of my marriage. Since I had established a relationship with her, I turned to Jocelyn once again. Though she did not specialize in circumstances like mine, she vowed to learn along with me. With her help, I could begin to take steps to reclaim my life and find a new normal.

I never imagined anything good could come from my divorce, but finding Jocelyn was certainly a gift. During our first session together, she asked me to name one friend, other than Chris, to whom I could go whenever I needed a listening ear. I immediately named my friend Wendy, who I worked with every day and who knew the current details of my life.

Enlisting the help of a trusted friend, who agreed to walk with me through those days, was an important step toward healing. Being able to share with Wendy also took some pressure off Chris to be my only source of comfort. What I didn't realize at the beginning was how the attack hurt Chris, too.

I wanted so much to try to continue living my life as normal. I wanted Chris to see the me that I used to be, but uncomfortable moments seemed to happen no matter where I went or what I did. Triggers were everywhere. I might see someone who looked like one of the attackers, or someone walking up behind me would startle me and send me into a panic.

Chris and I went out to celebrate his birthday, exactly a month after the attack, and the sight of a police officer and the gun in his holster was a trigger that sent both Chris and me into an emotional tailspin.

By October 22, I had been living at Chris's home for six weeks, and I was growing more and more concerned about the arrangement. I didn't want to move out, but I was also keenly aware that we wouldn't have been living together if not for the attack. I wondered when I would be ready to move out on my own again, but I couldn't figure out how to talk to Chris about it. I wanted so much to protect Chris from all the horrific details of the rape.

In my journal, I tried to figure out how to navigate my relationship with Chris in light of the abduction: *I wouldn't even be living here if it were not for what happened to me. I am afraid to be without him. When do I tell him what happened? Will I be ready? I am sick, and I want to shelter him from any hurt. He deserves a happy life, and I would love to have that with him."*

The very next day, I journaled about a conversation I had with my boss. I had begun to fear that I wasn't healing fast enough to keep from jeopardizing my job: *Talked to Ken about work and let him know how I was feeling and tried to inform him how I may take one step forward one day and two steps back the next. He was very understanding and thought I was doing a good job.*

On the same evening I wrote that entry, I wrote a letter to Art Billingsley and hoped to meet him so I could deliver it to him. In my journal, I recorded my thoughts, wondering if healing would ever fully come: *It was a hard letter to write, for it stirred up emotions—distinctly [the memory of] me tapping on my trunk in the moments before I was found.*

The entry ended with questions I wasn't sure how to answer and didn't know who to ask: *When will I look forward to an event or have something else on my mind? What will my life be like?*

As a runner, I know there is only one way to run a marathon: one step at a time. That, too, is the thing I would learn about healing. I simply had to keep putting one foot in front of the other. Some days it was harder than others.

The biggest difference between a marathon and my healing journey, however, is that a long race eventually has a finish line. But the healing journey doesn't ever really end. It is ongoing as long as we are alive, and its ripple effects go on far beyond even my own life.

I had to stop giving myself a timetable when I thought I should be "over it." There is no contest for speed or gracefulness in the messy work of healing. Those first stumbling steps were just the beginning, but they were steps in the right direction. I was learning who I could trust and figuring out how to ask for what I needed. And that was progress.

Chapter Eleven

Lifelines

I'm not interested in whether you've stood with the great. I'm interested in whether you've sat with the broken.

—The Age of Enlightenment

It would be easy to write a chapter about all the people whose words and actions were *not* helpful or to describe how hard it was to find people who could understand what it's like to come back from a tragedy like this. I found that my friendships changed a great deal. But as I began to move forward, I could see how *I* was the one who had changed.

My needs and perspective were totally redefined after that fateful night. As news of the attack made its way to more and more people, I received a lot of kind messages and notes from those whom I had known for many years. And though I was grateful for each thankful expression, I felt the need to distance myself from almost everyone for a while. Making it through each day took so much energy that I became easily overwhelmed.

I didn't mean to hurt or ignore the well-meaning people in my life, even family and close friends, whom I did not feel comfortable inviting into my pain. It was nothing personal. I just needed a sense of identity apart from what had happened to me.

There were, however, a few people and moments that became lifelines for me. I share this part of my story because, whether we know it or not, we all *need* lifelines at some point in our lives. And we will likely have the chance to *be* a lifeline to someone else, too.

Once you have received the gift of support from another human being during a difficult time, you understand more acutely the importance of being that lifeline for someone else when the tables are turned. I might never have known how to help someone find healing after a violent assault unless it happened to me first.

Whether someone is facing a trauma similar to mine or dealing with a loss, disappointment, health challenge, transition, or other life-changing event, your presence during a person's darkest days are more important than you can possibly imagine. Every word you say takes on unique importance when someone feels fragile because they are hearing everything through their layers of pain.

To be honest, I couldn't have anticipated ever becoming the lifeline for anyone else back then. I was not ready. I was in survival mode for months and really for the entire three years it took to walk through the legal proceedings. But paying attention to how others helped and what I needed during that time unknowingly educated me on how to become a lifeline for others in the future.

Of course, the first lifeline who showed up for me was Detective Arthur Billingsley, who was the only person who actually saw me while I was gagged, bound, and crammed in my car trunk. That moment when I was found was the first moment my suffering was acknowledged with compassion after the brutal attack. I will forever be grateful for Arthur's heart. Because of who he is and how he listened to his gut and took one more watchful drive through his community, my life was spared.

Arthur didn't stop with finding me, though. He stayed in my life and checked on me as often as he was able. Because the criminal justice system was seeking conviction for the attackers, Art had to be cautious and limit his contact with me throughout the legal process. Witnesses and law enforcement personnel were urged to cease communication for the integrity of the trials. But I knew he was never far away. I felt—and still feel—grateful that people like Art are serving and protecting my community.

During the year that followed the attack, Arthur Billingsley took confidentiality seriously. One day I saw him at the grocery store, and he introduced me to Leslie, the woman who would eventually become his wife. He refused to tell her how we knew one another until I finally begged him to tell her so she would not worry about who I was or why I held him in such high regard. They would both become cherished friends in the years to come.

I was grateful for my family, who stayed close and helped in so many ways. I'm sure it could sound cliché to say that my mom was a lifeline, but it's true. She provided support in practical ways that seem to come naturally to moms. She cooked for me often and worried that I wasn't eating enough. I stayed with her numerous times when I was afraid of being alone while Chris had to travel. She was my greatest cheerleader, and she still is. I remain grateful that she was, and always is, in my corner.

Lisa, my sister, was someone I could lean on anytime I needed her. She had a family of her own but always found ways to be there for me and help with whatever I needed. I stayed with her, too, whenever I needed the company of family. I never realized, when we were growing up, how much we would go through together as adults. I'll always be grateful for her.

Chris's sister, Mary, was also a tremendous support in many ways. When I had to do difficult things during the day, like going to look at police photos or other such dreaded tasks, Mary would accompany me to the police station and served as a comforting presence. Knowing how difficult it was for me to be alone, Mary gave me a guardian angel charm that was personalized for me. I still wear it on certain occasions when I need extra courage.

My therapist, Jocelyn, did not specialize in cases like mine, but she became a student of sexual assault on my behalf. She could have easily referred me to someone else, but she somehow knew how difficult it would be for me to establish trust with a new therapist in my traumatized condition. She bravely stepped up to the challenge, and I will forever be grateful for her willingness to do so.

It probably goes without saying that Chris was a lifeline. He was right there every moment, experiencing the very worst with me. Looking back, I now see how important it was that he started going to therapy, too. Not only did he need support to better equip himself to understand what the trauma had done to me, but he also needed help understanding how to get through it himself. It was important for both of us that he get perspective and guidance from someone trained to help people navigate these incredibly difficult circumstances.

I always recommend that family members of victims find lifelines, too, because nothing prepares you for the way trauma will affect your closest relationships, both at the time of the crisis and for the years that follow.

I read a book during the summer after the attack that became a lifeline. It was a book written by an assault survivor whose story became a manual of sorts that would give me hope that I could, in fact, survive this. Her book helped me believe a happy, fulfilling life was possible after trauma.

The friend Jocelyn asked me to name, Wendy, would walk with me and serve as a compassionate voice of comfort. She would also become a defender in many ways, particularly during the trials.

Wendy prepared a letter and document for the judge before the first sentencing that acknowledged my suffering. Her observations helped shed light on the way the scars of a violent trauma are not nearly as invisible as I thought.

In her letter, she included the following comparison between the version of me she observed before the attack and the version she saw afterward.

The old Michelle was always smiling; the new Michelle never smiled.

The old Michelle was always boisterous when she talked; the new Michelle was so quiet you had to strain to hear her when she talked.

The old Michelle had a contagious laugh; the new Michelle never laughed.

The old Michelle walked with her head high, her step bouncy and energetic; the new Michelle walked with her head down, her shoulders inward, her step void of energy.

The old Michelle would look in the mirror and be happy with herself; the new Michelle never even looked in the mirror.

The old Michelle was always the first to say, "Hello, how are you?" to everyone she passed in the hall; the new Michelle said nothing [to anyone] unless spoken to first.

The old Michelle kept her office door open; the new Michelle kept her office door closed.

The old Michelle was confident in her relationship with her partner, Chris; the new Michelle questioned her partner and their relationship.

The old Michelle cared about everyone every day, it seemed; the new Michelle sometimes didn't care about anyone any day, including herself.

The old Michelle worked long hours at her job, many times in the office late at night alone in the building; the new Michelle many times couldn't work an hour and was sometimes compelled to lock the entrance door closest to her office during normal business hours when other employees were present.

The old Michelle had a car trunk full of things; the new Michelle couldn't even open her car trunk.

The old Michelle loved to do things on her own; the new Michelle couldn't do anything on her own.

The old Michelle would walk in and out of a store, her home, the office, wherever, alone, without thinking a thing about it; the new Michelle couldn't walk anywhere alone.

The old Michelle slept often and sound; the new Michelle rarely slept, and when she did, she was plagued by nightmares.

The old Michelle never cried; the new Michelle spent the better part of many days doing nothing but crying.

The old Michelle was in control of her life and destiny; the new Michelle sometimes felt she had no control and was unsure if she had a destiny.

The old Michelle loved life and cherished it; the new Michelle often hated life and questioned it.

In her letter, she implored the judge to consider the ways these men's actions had impacted my life and to allow their sentences to reflect that reality. But, just as important, Wendy reminded me that I was seen, that what happened to me mattered, and that the pain wasn't just carried by me but by everyone who cared about me.

For a while I did not know how to reengage with the people who had been my lifelines before the attack. It was unlike me to not reach out to my close friends, but for several days, Sara and Amy, my friends since grade school, had been calling Chris to check on me. He told them I would be in touch as soon as I was able. But the truth is, I was afraid. I didn't know how to be the "me" they knew. That is one regret I have, but at the time, I kept waiting for the old me to reemerge so I didn't feel so strange and unlike the version of me they knew.

Finally, a couple of weeks after the attack, we connected, and they were amazing. I didn't know what to say and feared our friendship might somehow change because of what had happened to me. The moment we were together again, my fears melted away. They were concerned about me, of course, but their friendship was steadying for me because it was another step toward understanding that life and friendship could be good again. Sara and Amy remain lifelines to this day.

That day, Sara told me a story I've never forgotten that happened on the night of the attack. She and her husband,

Nate, were out of town celebrating his birthday with their family. They were staying in a condo and watching a movie with the kids, but she couldn't concentrate on the movie. She was feeling uneasy and kept checking the windows, finding that they wouldn't lock. Nate came into the bedroom, asking what the heck she was doing, and he couldn't get them to lock either. She couldn't shake the eerie feeling or explain it. She just knew something felt wrong—unsafe. She was sure her kids and husband thought she was crazy, but she couldn't shake it.

The next day, she heard the news of my attack and realized her uneasiness happened during the exact time I was fighting for my life. That is the kind of friends Amy and Sara are. We are deeply connected, and our friendship has sustained us through many seasons, both painful and joyful.

I can't imagine trying to survive this kind of horrific experience without these lifelines God put into my path. Their presence helped me find myself again. There are so many other amazing people who supported me in countless ways and for whom I am deeply grateful. The Acknowledgments of this book offer a glimpse at the incredible community of people I have to thank.

Chapter Twelve

Getting Past the Past

Owning our own story and loving ourselves
through that process is the bravest thing
we'll ever do.
—Brené Brown

The horror of being abducted and assaulted was deeply wounding, which isn't surprising. But I would learn that trauma also has a strange way of stirring up old wounds.

Pain I thought was behind me resurfaced at what felt like the most inopportune time. Things like abandonment and loss of trust that happened earlier in life—first from my father and later during my divorce—had to be dealt with at a new level in order to heal emotionally. These old wounds were invisible but very present under the surface.

Turns out, the brain remembers trauma, and the body reacts to it until we are able to identify the source and gain an understanding of how it has ravaged our inner life.

I never knew the security of a loving dad. That abandonment so early in life left a mark on my soul that I had not fully realized or expressed until I faced this crisis. It was a wound from which no one could protect me and something no one could fix. All the romance, success, or great moments in the world do not erase the questions and longings that come with being fatherless. Yet that wound seemed to lie dormant until opened up by other life events. I see now that it wasn't really dormant. The underlying reality of that wound had informed my decisions and thought processes all along, but I didn't have the tools or awareness to identify it.

At twenty-one, I married someone I met in high school. He became my escape from all the things I felt were wrong in my life. Like me, he was raised Catholic and came from a nice family. He had money in the bank and promised to take care of me. I considered him my knight in shining armor.

I longed to be loved so much that I ignored warning signals that might have kept me from years of torment. He was charming and told me everything I wanted to hear. He made promises about a lifetime together that he was not able to fulfill. Day after day, year after year, I talked myself out of my mistrust and questions about him that came up over and over again. I really loved him, and I was convinced we could make it through anything. But

I couldn't change the fact that the person I hoped and believed I was marrying was not the person I actually married. His actions eventually convinced me that he had no intention—or at least no ability—to be the kind of devoted spouse he had led me to believe he was. I became disoriented, to say the least.

In time, I learned of illegal activity he was involved in, yet he had no intention of stopping. I couldn't live complicit in the harm being done to defenseless individuals. So I left him for the sake of those he was hurting and for my own safety.

He was unwilling to accept divorce, yet he was also unwilling to take responsibility for his actions, prolonging the divorce until the relationship became unbearably messy. He wasn't interested in his own healing or mine. After a brutal year-and-a-half of standing my ground, the marriage was legally dissolved. The healing, however, took much longer.

We'd bought a house next to a church, which turned out to be a blessing. I often walked over to the church during those dark, tumultuous days. I found solace there, just like when I was a little girl. Those peaceful moments inside the walls of the church, as well as hundreds of prayers for safety and guidance, offered quiet respite that I desperately needed.

I was plagued with confusion. I didn't know whether or not divorcing in this scenario was forgivable—even after he had multiple affairs. He capitalized on my desire to do the right thing, insisting that we were married, for better or for worse, and that I was breaking our vows. But I finally determined "worse" didn't mean I had to participate in the kind of life he chose to live. He, too, had broken vows to be faithful and to love, honor, and cherish me.

The divorce was a horrible part of my life. I felt I had lost everything. The loneliness was profound. There were days and nights of endless tears and guilt. I had always believed that God wouldn't give me more than I could handle, but I believed this was *the* test of my life—that *this* was my tough time. I couldn't imagine anything more difficult. So I believed if only I could get beyond it, there would only be good in the future. If I passed that test with flying colors, I wouldn't have to feel that kind of pain again. Oh, how wrong I was.

Not having a father figure in my life was beyond my control, but I had *chosen* this man to grow old with. I'd trusted this man with my life and my future—until I finally realized that I didn't even know him, much less the hurt he was capable of bringing into my life and the lives of others.

How could I have had such poor judgment? Why couldn't I see these concerning signs earlier in the relationship? Where had I gone wrong? I had to confront myself and grapple with questions about life as never before.

The truth is, he made sure I couldn't see those dark secrets he was hiding. He had become highly skilled at distracting me from any doubts I might have felt. I would learn that when people hurt us, placing all the blame on ourselves is not productive or healing; however, we *can* use those experiences to become wiser. We *can* nurture our ability to understand ourselves and deepen our trust in our instincts.

I am convinced that, even when our lives become a tangled mess because of human error, every circumstance we face can either send us into hiding or help us develop parts of ourselves we would not otherwise attend to. My eyes needed to be opened in order to free myself from abuse, betrayal, and darkness.

When our eyes are opened, we don't always like what we see, but only then can we deal with the realities in front of us. Pain and evil seem to lie in wait when we least expect them. Yet, living in fear of them is wasted energy. I would rediscover life and joy after the divorce, and I would gain valuable coping skills that I would need for the rest of my life. But there were days it was hard to imagine how any good could ever come of it.

Carrying all the baggage and disappointment of the past certainly caused me to proceed with extreme caution when Chris began to pursue me. During the months preceding the attack, most of the time we had spent together was about building trust. I let him do most of the talking because I needed to know what I was getting into. I didn't want to ignore any warning signs this time because I never wanted to repeat the agony I went through during the divorce.

In spite of Chris's patience, gentleness, and faithful friendship before and after the attack—even allowing me to stay in his home for several months—I began to feel that I needed to *know* I could live on my own again. I didn't want to end up with Chris by default. I didn't want to go on living with the fear of being independent. I didn't fully know where the relationship was going, and I needed some space to figure out what I needed. I had leaned on him so heavily during those months following the assault that I was worried my judgment was impaired.

I'm sure he, too, had questions about the future of our relationship. And we certainly weren't getting any clarity during those brutal nine months that followed the attack. I had pushed him away over and over again as a result of all the trauma, all the years of being disappointed by men in my life, and all the pain that had built up. But he wouldn't leave me. He only got upset at me one time, and even then, he was upset on my behalf and wanted me to believe in myself more.

I felt like he needed to know exactly what happened to me. I wrote out all the details of the attack, things he wondered but never pressed me to tell him, and I allowed him to read it. He didn't react, saying that it was enough for him to know that I was sexually assaulted. At first that made me angry, too, but he kept patiently staying with me no matter what I tried to do to see if he would leave me.

The attack would forever change my ability to be intimate. I felt guilty about that and about so many other things that I almost expected him to give up on me at some point. But he refused to stop loving me.

Though the need to prove my independence was completely self-inflicted, Chris never begged me to stay. So I began looking for another place to live.

By summer, I had begun teaching group fitness classes again at a local facility, and I met a friend there who managed an apartment complex. She invited me to a cookout hosted by the apartment management. The gathering offered tenants a chance to socialize and potential tenants an opportunity to learn more about the apartment community. I reluctantly agreed to attend since I was determined to find a place where I could feel safe. I thought this might be the answer.

After arriving, I found a seat in the poolside area and began to observe the people who might become my neighbors. As I looked around at the unfamiliar faces, I saw the face of a young police officer whom I recognized. It was Arthur Billingsley!

We greeted one another, and I asked him what brought him to this event. To my delight, he told me he watched over this apartment complex in his off-duty hours. He went on to say that he would be moving into the complex soon.

This news was incredibly relieving to me. I took it as a clear sign that I would be safe here and that this move could be a good thing. I didn't want to run away from anything or anyone, but I did want to move forward in my own healing. For me, healing involved reclaiming my sense of independence.

That summer, before I moved out of Chris's home and into the apartment complex, I read a book I'd sought out at the library: *Within a Dark Wood* by Jennifer Barr. Jennifer was the survivor of a violent attack similar to mine. I didn't realize until reading her story that the feelings I had on my drive home from the hospital, wishing for someone to come into my path who could understand what I was going through, indicated that I wanted to live. Even feelings that seemed negative and unpleasant at the time were important coping mechanisms. My mind and body were looking for ways to survive, and her book showed me that it was possible.

Her honesty about her story helped me understand my own, and I was relieved to learn that she experienced a range of emotions similar to how I'd felt. Her book became the most affirming book I'd ever read up to that point in my life. It was a blessing to discover it at such a crucial point in my life. Her story gave me hope that I would not always feel like a victim but a survivor, who could go on to enjoy a full, meaningful life.

While my first instinct had been to try to "get over it" as quickly as possible, I discovered that you never fully "get over" trauma. The way I had reacted to people and circumstances after the attack didn't mean I was crazy. In fact, every feeling I experienced was totally normal. Before living with the aftereffects of the attack, I never understood how trauma changes the brain's wiring. Triggers send impulses to a part of the brain that overrides all rational thoughts with a "fight or flight" reaction. That is why the sight of shrubbery dropped me to my knees on an otherwise normal afternoon stroll. Understanding this was powerfully liberating.

Moving past the things that have hurt us isn't about denying or forgetting the reality of what has happened. That simply isn't impossible. And it isn't about running away from the pain because our pain comes with us everywhere we go. Getting past the past, for me, became a journey of acceptance that my story was forever changed by trauma. But it was still my story, not anyone else's. I could find my voice again when I realized I'd never actually lost it. I simply had to rediscover it. I needed time to relearn how to be *me* in this new reality.

Moving out of Chris's house was ultimately a good decision, but my first night in the new apartment was terrifying. I knew the time had come for me to accept the reality of all that had happened and decide what a hopeful future might look like, with or without Chris.

Chapter Thirteen

The Fight for Justice

*Vulnerability is not winning or losing; it's having
the courage to show up and be seen when we
have no control over the outcome.*

—Brené Brown

For three years, I felt as if my life was on hold. Three years is how long it took for the Trunk Rapists' trials and sentencing to transpire. The pursuit of justice began immediately with the brutal rape kit I endured to gather evidence. The first attacker, whom Detective Billingsley handcuffed before freeing me from the trunk, was arrested that night and charged with criminal confinement and resisting law enforcement.

On Friday, September 13, the day after my attack, the second attacker was arrested at his home and charged with criminal confinement, aiding in rape, aiding in criminal deviate conduct, aiding in armed carjacking, conspiracy to commit armed robbery, and resisting law enforcement.

The third attacker was found at a relative's house around four-thirty on Friday afternoon. He was charged with criminal confinement, aiding in rape, aiding in criminal deviate conduct, aiding in armed carjacking, conspiracy to commit armed robbery, and resisting arrest.

On Saturday, September 14, Fort Wayne's *Journal Gazette* featured a story that revealed details about my attack that shocked me. While my name was not used in the story, it was hard to accept that my family and friends would read the story and know embarrassing facts that I was not comfortable sharing with anyone yet.

In that same report, Police Chief T. Neil Moore verified that detectives were investigating the attackers' probable connection to the other violent attacks in the area. Some of the other women's attacks were committed by only two men, while others involved all three.

The investigation did, in fact, uncover evidence implicating their guilt in the other local attacks. The first court dates were focused on the other victims, whose attacks happened before mine. I would learn, through those trials, what the other women endured.

The first known attack occurred on Thursday, August 15, 1996—four weeks prior to their final attack on me—and involved two women in their early twenties. They were parked at a bar when two men forced themselves into their car. The men claimed they had car trouble and asked the women to drive them to an apartment complex. But once they arrived at the complex, one of the men produced a gun. He forced one of the women into the trunk of the car and placed a plastic bag over the head of the other woman. The men drove them to a field and raped them repeatedly; then, the men sent them off without clothes or the car.

The women ran on foot through a wooded area, swam across the St. Joseph River, and then crossed through a corn field before approaching a house where they stopped for help. When the homeowner opened his door, he found the two panicky women naked, sobbing, and out of breath. He testified in court that the women told him they had been raped and named one of the attackers. One of the victims was able to positively identify one of her attackers because he lit a match in her face.

The second attack occurred on Sunday, September 1, 1996, just after midnight in the parking lot of a Fort Wayne apartment complex. A woman was accosted and forced into the trunk of her car by two men, one of whom was carrying a gun. Somehow, from inside the trunk, the victim was able to free herself and jump out of the vehicle while it was stopped at a traffic light. The suspects pursued her, but a passer-by picked her up and drove her to safety.

An hour later, on September 1, a Fort Wayne woman in her twenties returned to her apartment around one in the morning after visiting friends in nearby Lake James. She parked her car in the lot behind her apartment building. Just after she got out of her car, one man approached her and hit her above her right eye with a gun. Then he and a second attacker stole her keys and forced her into the trunk of her car.

They left her in the vehicle's trunk for about twenty minutes while they ransacked her apartment. When they returned to the car, they took her back to her apartment where they both took turns raping her. During this time, the men covered their faces so only their eyes showed. She recalled passing out a few times. One of the men forced her to sit in a bathtub after the rapes in an effort to remove evidence.

Since the woman's car had a manual transmission and neither attacker knew how to drive it, they gave her the option of driving them where they wanted to go or throwing her in the trunk again. At gunpoint, they led her back to her car, toting several items they had stolen from her apartment, including a videocassette recorder, some CDs, and loose change she had stored in a jar. By this time, both attackers were no longer disguising themselves. They forced her to drive to Fort Wayne's inner city and drop them off in an alley. She then drove herself to a hospital where police responded to a call about the incident around three o'clock in the morning. In court, she was able to identify both attackers.

The fourth attack to the fifth victim occurred on Saturday, September 7, 1996, in Bloomington, Indiana. A twenty-one-year-old Indiana University student was attacked inside her apartment by two men who entered through her unlocked door. She had just arrived home a few minutes before ten o'clock at night and left the door unlocked for her roommate. The attackers struck her over the head with what she guessed was a metal pipe or gun, blindfolded her, bound her, and covered her mouth with duct tape. She was robbed, and then the two attackers took her car keys and attempted to put her in the trunk, but she broke free and ran to a fraternity house for help.

I was eager to talk with these women about surviving this kind of violence, but we were not allowed to discuss the details of our attacks with each other. I was only able to interact with the other Trunk Rapists' victims after the trials were complete and with the help of our victim advocate, Pat Smallwood. My desire to find someone who had experienced a similar trauma was thwarted. Despite having been brutalized by the same three men, we could not find solace in one another in the interest of seeking justice. The other victims couldn't be the confidants I needed.

Each of the women was dealing with the trauma in her own way. Overall, I felt deep compassion for each of the other survivors, prayed for them, and hoped they had the support they needed. It was a frustrating reality that the only people who would surely understand my pain were off limits.

Each victim of crime has the opportunity to write a victim impact statement that is presented to the judge at sentencing. You can choose to read it out loud or simply present the written copy to the judge. I chose to read mine out loud. While I was in court preparing to read my statement, I noticed there was handwriting at the top of the page. It was in Chris's handwriting and simply read, *I can do all things through Christ who strengthens me* (Philippians 4:13).

I held on to this verse over and over again. I leaned on the peace I'd experienced when I thought I would die in my trunk. I held to the belief that, somehow, I could get through this. And I chose to believe my life had been spared for a reason. So I kept going. I knew that the strength I had was not all my own. Philippians 4:13 is still a verse I depend on daily to face whatever is in front of me.

I was the sixth woman to be targeted and, thanks to Arthur Billingsley and the law enforcement team who stopped them, the last of the Trunk Rapists' victims. But, because I did not see my attackers' faces, I could not visually identify them in court. This unfortunate fact made my case more difficult to prove than the others. Court dates were postponed multiple times, and the resolution I longed for was prolonged again and again. The waiting was excruciating. Every court appearance would bring me face-to-face with the pain, the humiliation, and the fear, not to mention the faces and voices of my attackers.

Each time I had to recount the events of that night, I would go right back to that brutal series of events and reopen the wound. Every court date felt like I was being brutalized all over again. Having to choose between personal healing and public safety feels like a no-win scenario during the legal process. I could only hope serving justice would be worth the personal price I, along with the other women, paid.

We don't always think about how much the fight for justice affects not only the survivors but also their loved ones. Sitting through testimonies was devastating to Chris. Hearing the humiliating details of the brutality these men inflicted on me, and in such a public setting, was brutal. He, too, struggled to look into their faces. Having him there, along with my family, throughout the entire ordeal meant the world to me, especially knowing how difficult the experience was for them.

The newspaper and media were there in full force, too, for more top stories, with all the disturbing and personal details of the attacks retold in brutal detail with every story. It was difficult not to feel completely paralyzed at times. And the trials inevitably brought some scary relapses of fear and PTSD episodes.

On October 22, 1997, over a year after my attack, the first of my three attackers pled guilty. He was sentenced to seventy years in prison the following January.

The second attacker's trial was scheduled for January 20, 1998, and to our disappointment, the trial was postponed until May 2, 1998, which was a disheartening development. I, along with Chris and my family, would prepare mentally to be in the room with someone who had caused so much pain, only to learn that we would have to wait months longer. Over and over again, we felt the emotional impact of not having resolution.

During sentencing, the judge said he "had never heard something so cruel and so vicious" during his legal career. He gave our attacker the maximum sentence for the seven felony convictions—the longest sentence that had ever been handed down in Allen County, barring life without parole. His sentences were consecutive, meaning they would be served one after another, for a total of three hundred twenty years.

This attacker had said in a recorded interview, "I just want to say I really feel sorry for these victims, and I hope they really find the people that did it."

Deputy Prosecutor Karen Richardson had to quell her anger at this outrage of an apology. She told the judge she had never seen a crime so vicious, humiliating, or degrading in her seventeen years in the prosecutor's office, stating, "What [he] did to these two women tells me we have reached a new low in the way one individual treats another. The actions of these men remind me of a pack of wild animals, running together and feeding off a frenzy."

He showed no emotion during the hearing and shook his head *no* when one of his victims told him an apology would "help me a lot."

Soon after, I got word that the third trial was going to be postponed again. It had already been postponed to October 21, 1997. I had endured a grueling pretrial rehearsal in which I had to review the events of the entire evening of the attack and look at photographs taken by police. And though I knew what had happened, nothing quite prepared me for how it would feel to see crime scene photos of my belongings scattered in front of my home and blood from my head wound on the floor. It was shocking. Yet, as difficult as it was, I was determined to keep him from hurting anyone else.

On the evening of October 20, I got word that there might be another postponement and I needed to show up at the courthouse the next morning at eight-thirty. When I arrived the next morning, I was nervous. My body shook as we stood outside the courtroom, waiting and wondering what would happen next. Then, our victim assistant, Pat Smallwood, delivered the news that we were postponed again until June unless I accepted the final attacker's plea.

As it turned out, he decided to plead guilty. My first response was, "No way!"

Pat then explained the details of the plea and what it would mean. I learned that accepting the plea would mean I did not have to get on the stand and retell the details of that night. Pat also felt that accepting the plea would keep us from risking a jury finding him not guilty since I did not get a good look at his face during the attack.

Chris and I stepped aside to discuss our options. I needed time to think and pray before I could reach a decision. I was afraid. I didn't want to feel like I had lost—like I was failing—by accepting a plea. By early afternoon, I decided to take the plea.

As soon as I accepted the plea, I knew it was a good decision for me. I immediately felt relief flood my body and mind. I knew I would need to face him again in court to hear his plea and for sentencing, but I also knew that doing so would allow me to hear him admit the wrong he had done against me.

Chris, Lisa, and my mom came to the sentencing the following day. When we walked into the courtroom, my attacker was already seated. He was wearing an orange jumpsuit and was chained and handcuffed. As we made our way to our seats, he stared at Chris and me. My stomach felt sick, but I refused to give him the satisfaction of knowing I was bothered by his presence. I did not want to be intimidated by him any longer. I knew what he was about to tell the judge and needed to hear him say it. I sat next to Chris and, at times, squeezed his hand so hard I thought I might break his fingers. I was so angry that I almost felt like I could punch him so he could feel some of the pain and humiliation he had caused me.

When the attacker's time came to speak, I sat up with the prosecutor, Karen, and Pat. I looked at him, and he looked back. My body shuddered again.

He proceeded to plead guilty to one count of rape, one count of aiding kidnapping, and one count of conspiracy to commit robbery. Initially, he hedged, saying he and some friends "supposedly" kidnapped the woman.

Superior Court Judge John F. Surbeck Jr. immediately interrupted him, telling him he was not going to be allowed to be vague. He told the defendant to state what he had done.

He then admitted that on September 12, 1996, he "had sexual intercourse with an innocent bystander without her permission." He admitted to being involved, along with the other two men, whom he named, in my kidnapping, and he admitted that they also had conspired to rob the Bandidos restaurant.

His sentencing, scheduled for November, was postponed until January 5, 1998. Then, on the morning of January 5, 1998, I was able to walk into the courthouse and confront one of my attackers with the detailed aftermath of his crime. This time he was the one held captive with nothing to protect him from the reality of how his actions had impacted me.

The scariest thing about going to sentencing and facing your perpetrator is looking at him and hearing his witnesses' testimonies. This attacker even had a pastor come in and say, "He is a good boy. He is only nineteen."

The pastor explained to the judge that this young man wanted to get married and have a family. He asked him to give him a second chance—that he'd made a mistake.

In my impact statement, I pointed out that we can make a mistake, but he made five (referring to the other victims) and took away something from these women they would never get back.

He did eventually ask for forgiveness, claiming, "I'm not the same person as when I came in. I'm a changed man; I got myself right."

After his half-hearted apology, the judge stated that he remained unconvinced of the assailant's remorse.

With my family and friends by my side, I watched as he was sentenced to thirty years for rape, thirty years for aiding in kidnapping, and ten years for conspiring to commit robbery. As part of the plea, the state dropped charges of carjacking and resisting law enforcement.

The seventy-year sentence was far shy of the one hundred twenty-year sentence Deputy Prosecutor Richardson originally pursued but, for me, sentencing went better than expected. He may have only received half of what he deserved, but this part was over. Afterwards, there was only relief.

Four days later, the last assailant finally pled guilty to his involvement in my attack and the August 15 attack. The final court appearance I would have to make would be his hearing. I felt confident that the worst was behind us, and I already knew the attackers would be in prison for the rest of their lives. So, even with the last court date pending, I began to feel like I could breathe again.

The justice system is imperfect, for sure. And reliving the trauma was only possible because I knew it wasn't about me. The fight for justice was about more than fighting against those who committed crimes. It was about fighting *for* something bigger. I was fighting for the safety of women everywhere who have been brutalized and for a safer world.

I would discover that the best justice I could ever find was to survive this horrible experience and become better for it. That would be the best outcome and the one and only way not to let evil win.

Chapter Fourteen

The Fourth of July

Sometimes the dreams that come true are the dreams you never knew you had.

—Alice Sebold

For the entire span of our relationship, the circumstances swirling around Chris and me had been heavy. Just when he started to find his emotional equilibrium after his divorce, the abduction threw us into crisis mode at a level that made it hard to imagine how "normal life" might look.

Before the attack, we had developed a deep friendship and the ability to engage in meaningful, honest conversations. I respected his stability and thoughtfulness. We encouraged one another in our faith. But three years later, we were unsure how to recapture what we had before the attack. The pain we both experienced became an obstacle that forced us to prioritize our individual healing over our relationship.

Since Chris did most of the talking at the beginning of our relationship, processing all his thoughts and feelings about his divorce, he didn't have a full picture of my background. I liked him a lot. But I did all the listening for a reason. I didn't want to unpack my history until I knew he was someone I could trust with the good, the bad, and the ugly of my story.

A few months after the attack, we found ourselves sitting in a bar. Our future together was on the line. The voice running through my head was asking, *What are we doing? Are we going to do something here? Because if not, I'm moving on.*

During that conversation, Chris found himself saying out loud, "If you think I'm going to ask you to marry me right now, the answer is no."

Moving into my own apartment allowed me to reclaim my sense of self again. We began to go on dates and have conversations that did not revolve solely around our pain, the trauma, or the three-year-long judicial process.

He had proven his ability to stand by me and patiently support me, even when I wasn't able to reciprocate. But now, he was the one who needed to regain trust in me. He needed to know that I wouldn't reject him out of my own pain and self-protection.

A few weeks before the last trial, in July of 1998, we decided to spend the Fourth of July weekend at Crystal

Lake, Michigan, where a friend of ours owned a cabin. It was so good to get out of town and spend time in nature.

We started the Fourth of July weekend by participating in an early morning race. It felt so wonderful to just let myself run. I didn't try to keep pace with Chris; I let myself go as fast as I could. I was in my element. I wasn't trying to be competitive, but to my surprise, I finished third place in my age division.

We returned to the cabin later that morning, and the weather was beautiful. I decided to sit and soak up the sunshine while Chris took his dog, Cigar, for a boat ride on the lake. It felt good to enjoy peace again.

Later we went hiking on Sleeping Bear Dunes, and for the first time in a long time, I felt present and in the moment. It might have been the first time since the attack that I actually believed peace and happiness might be attainable after all that had happened. I was keenly aware of the beauty around us. The sky was brilliant blue; the water was clear and sparkling; and I felt content. I was grateful to be there with him.

Back at the cabin, after all the physical exercise that day, I was hungry. We showered and headed to a local restaurant for dinner. I noticed he didn't eat much, but it had been such a perfect day, I didn't overthink it. I was just enjoying being in this place with him.

We went back to the cabin where Chris packed a cooler, and we boarded the boat to watch fireworks on the lake. The sun had already set, and the fireworks were going to start soon, so Chris raced the boat to a perfect spot on the lake. Once he found our spot, he poured us each a glass of champagne and told me he had written something he wanted to read to me.

"Am I going to cry?" I asked, having no idea what he was up to.

He didn't answer but reached into his sweater, pulled out a small pad of paper, and began reciting a poem he had written:

My Michelle

My Michelle, we've come so far
From the day when we first met.
I think back about that fateful day
With remorse but no regret.
In black and gold with stars so bright,
You shined just like the sun.
How was I to ever know
That you would be the one?
We started slow because of me,
So anxious and afraid.
You stuck by me; you saw it through;
You wouldn't let it fade.
I remember all the times together,
Sitting on the floor.
We laughed and cried and shared our hearts.
Those moments most adored.
Just when things began to grow,
The past would come to haunt us.
But still we managed to find the way,

Our commitment was undaunted.
Then there came the worst of all
That dreadful night September.
A night so bad you try to forget,
But one you must remember.
Because through it all,
You've gained strength from Jesus Lord above
To handle all the trials of life
Through God's grace and love.
We battled through all the trouble
And conquered all the fear
By communicating with each other
And drawing forever near.
You've always shown such strength
And been a great example
Of how to treat and love another,
Your love always more than ample.
From Soldier Field to Wrigley,
The Komets in the Fort,
Festa, Marshall, and the
Bed and breakfast in Laporte.
From Florida's coasts, both east and west,
It's been a wonderful trip.
We've cruised the waters of the seas
And walked the Vegas strip.
Though we've done a lot and seen much more,
There's still so much to do.
I can't imagine a better way
Than to do it all with you.

Sometimes it seems so long ago,
Sometimes just yesterday,
When Jesus brought you in my life,
A place I hope you'll stay.
I profess to you my undying love,
Something I'm sure to repeat.
There's just one thing for me to do
To make my life complete.
I promise to make you happy;
That's all that I can do.
It really should be easy, though,
Because I'm so in love with you.
After everything that we've been through,
I know with whom I'm destined to be.
My Michelle, my dear Michelle,
Will you marry me?

I had been crying since the first two words he read: "My Michelle." His words in those moments were the most beautiful words I had ever heard.

I did not leave him in suspense: "Yes! Oh, my gosh, yes!"

I was totally shocked, especially after the conversation we had earlier in the year. He still reminds me that he said, "If you think I'm going to ask you to marry me *right now*." He had apparently been planning this moment for a while, but I couldn't have been more surprised and overjoyed.

He then gave me a ring that took my breath away. Not only was it beautiful, but it also represented everything in our lives that had brought us to this moment. I knew without a doubt that we belonged together, not just because of the emotions I experienced in that moment but because I knew in the very depths of me that he and I were better together. We had already survived so much that I knew we could handle whatever else life might bring.

That night felt like a dream—a wonderful, perfect dream. The fireworks on that Fourth of July paled in comparison to the explosion of joy and gratitude happening in my heart.

On the ride home, I couldn't stop smiling. My gaze moved back and forth between Chris and the ring on my finger. I felt like the luckiest girl alive.

We got back to Fort Wayne late at night, but I couldn't wait another moment to tell my mom and sister. I had to tell them in person, so we delivered the news face-to-face. They were overjoyed. They, too, had seen the way Chris stayed by my side during the worst of the worst.

I couldn't wait to tell the world.

Chapter Fifteen

Hope Deferred

When the world says give up, hope whispers,
try it one more time.

—King Tutankhamun

A few weeks before the final sentencing, I opened the newspaper and saw the headline: "State Seeks to Drop Some Charges against Rapist." As I read the story, I realized the article was announcing the state's plan to drop the charges against the man with the soft voice for attacking me on September 12th.

Because of his voice, even without seeing his face, I knew he was the one who struck me on the head with his gun, demanded my wallet, bound my hands and blindfolded me, and instructed the other two attackers throughout that terrible night. Yet he was the only one of my three attackers who would not serve a single moment for his part in my attack. He had already been sentenced to three hundred twenty years in prison for his part in the other crimes against women, so the state decided not to pursue a sentence for my attack.

I was crushed. My disappointment in the judicial system was somehow made worse because I read this news in the paper rather than hearing it in the courtroom where I could express my disheartenment.

My final court date was scheduled for July 21, 1998. That day would determine the sentence for my second attacker, but after the disappointing news on the ring leader's participation in my attack, I went into that day with utter discouragement, but clung to hope that justice would be served for this attacker, too.

Every court date was traumatizing. Every time I was brought face-to-face with these criminals, along with their families and friends, I had to relive what happened on the night that changed the course of my life. I always faced the question of how any amount of justice could ever be enough.

The second attacker had already pled guilty, but still I longed to see him receive the maximum sentence. During his sentencing, he made a half-hearted attempt at apologizing and requested leniency. Claiming he had no clue what caused him to commit these crimes, he stated that he felt less than a man to stand before the court without an explanation. Although he admitted it was his turn to suffer, he also asked for another chance at life. He even went as far as to say, "I'm not a bad person. I'm not. I just done a bad thing . . . I don't think I deserve to die in prison."

Throughout the entire judicial process for all three attackers, Deputy Prosecutor Karen Richardson had repeatedly emphasized that these men gave up the right to walk among any decent human beings when they became sexual predators.

I sat confidently and boldly and told the judge what he had done to me. I explained to him how the events of that night impacted my life on so many levels. I insisted he receive the maximum sentence. I felt strong and determined not to let him control my peace of mind any longer.

"I don't think I have ever seen anything worse," the prosecutor stated.

This attacker had already been sentenced to one hundred sixty years in prison for his involvement in the August 15 attack of the two young women. But during this final sentencing, we listened as the verdict was handed down that he would serve another fifty years for his involvement in my attack. This sentence would run consecutively with the two hundred ten years he had already received. He would never again appear on a sidewalk at night as a hooded predator seeking prey.

Two victims of previous attacks were in the courtroom when the verdict was handed down. They wiped tears and shook visibly upon hearing his sentence.

With the stringent sentences the other attackers received, I was confident none of them would ever walk free again. I felt fortunate they would never be eligible for parole. So many survivors never hear that.

When all the trials were over, the reality was that only two of my three assailants would spend time in jail for raping me. The clear ring leader—the man with the soft voice, who begged for leniency—would receive no sentence for what he did to me, despite statements by the other two attackers implicating him.

The charges against him in my case were officially dropped, leaving the impression that he was innocent. This man would serve only fifty years—concurrent with his other sentences—not for the charge of rape but rather for criminal confinement, which he admitted to in his taped interview and in his plea.

Chris, too, was relieved that the trials and court dates were all behind us, and he was glad these men would never walk free, but he later expressed his lingering sadness over the way the judicial system failed to fully serve justice for their crimes against me:

If you think about the heinous nature of the crimes against Michelle—coupled with the fact they had been on this rampage and done it a number of times previously and the violence continued to escalate—not one of these guys was ever tried and put away for anything they did to Michelle. Even though they captured [the first assailant] and he confessed and implicated the other two, even though they found blood evidence and credit card activity implicating the other two, since there was no positive identification, they didn't feel like they could prosecute them. Maybe it was because they'd be put away for a long time for their other crimes, but that doesn't help Michelle. As a victim—it's all well and good for the other victims—but what about her? Where is her closure and the accountability for what they did to her?

I understand there may be many pragmatic reasons for dropping charges against someone, such as saving taxpayer money. Perhaps, when a criminal is already sentenced to consecutive life sentences for crimes against other people in a series of similar crimes, a prosecutor has nothing to gain by having another trial. What would another life sentence really accomplish, especially if the victim never saw her attacker's face? But that additional life *did* matter to me. Because *my* life mattered. My well-being mattered. This, the justice system ignored. This hurt, deeply.

Despite the pain this caused me, my family, and friends, knowing it was all over left me relieved and exhilarated. I'll never forget standing on the courthouse steps side-by-side with Chris, my family, and friends in those momentous moments following the last sentencing. "Freedom" seemed to emanate from the expressions on our faces. Half of me was overjoyed that it was over, yet half of me understood we would never feel like anything made it all okay.

Someone even took photos before we departed, and I'm so glad we have them. Looking back on that memory now is so significant.

On that sunny July day, I finally turned my back on the courthouse, descended the steps, and went on with my life. I went directly from there to shop for a wedding dress. I was finally ready to accept what *was,* however painful and imperfect, and step into a new chapter of my life that was full of hope.

Chapter Sixteen

Becoming Mrs. Corrao

*Happiness cannot be traveled to, owned, earned,
worn, or consumed. Happiness is the spiritual
experience of living every minute with love,
grace, and gratitude.*

—Denis Waitley

Chris and I were married on November 14, 1998.
We started planning for a small, intimate wedding
and ended up having two hundred fifty people
join us for this joyful day.

At the rehearsal the night before our wedding, I
remember looking around the church, surrounded by
all my family and friends, and feeling overwhelmed with
happiness. Every person there was truly happy for Chris
and me, and we felt tremendously grateful for their love

and support. It is easy to show up for someone on their happiest days, but these were the people who had been there on our worst days, too. I would come to see how suffering can bring gifts if we allow ourselves to see them, including the people who surround us and hold us up.

The wedding could not have been more perfect. It was the fairy tale wedding of my dreams.

My dress was the first one I tried on after leaving the courthouse on July 21. I found it on the clearance rack, and it was everything I wanted. I still love that dress and put it on every year on our anniversary.

It was a perfect day. Chris even arranged for a limo to take me and my family to the church.

At the reception, Chris surprised me with another poem he'd written:

I Raise This up to You

My Michelle, my dear Michelle,
You did marry me.
I'm so proud to have you as my wife,
To spend my years with thee.
Our engagement had indeed been short;
The days they seemed so few.
Do this; plan that; write another check.
You're inviting who?
But everything has come together,
Just like we knew it would.
This day is blessed by heaven
As only Jesus could,

A day of utmost beauty,
An emotional release
Filled with style and elegance,
With you the centerpiece.
I look forward to all our years together,
The good times and the bad,
Adding to the scrapbook
Of memories that we've had.
So, together with our families
And all our friends, so true,
With all my heart and all my love,
I raise this toast to you!

Later, I tried to capture my thoughts in my journal:

All I can say is, what a night. It was a fairy tale, a dream come true. It was everything. I couldn't believe it was me living it. Of all women, Chris chose me. I think every woman at the reception fell for Chris when he made his toast. Chris, your love amazes me! I'll never stop thanking you for the happiness you have brought into my life.

The next morning, I woke up early and ran five miles. I couldn't stop thanking God that I would get to spend the rest of my life with Chris.

We waited until January to celebrate our honeymoon in Hawaii. It felt good to get settled a bit after the wedding so we could enjoy the time away.

Leaving the Indiana winter to explore the beauty of Hawaii brought us many moments of gratitude, much like those peaceful moments we experienced at Crystal Lake on our engagement day. At times, I felt like I needed to pinch myself to be sure this was really my life. It was a long way from Fort Wayne and from all we had survived together.

Our first year of marriage brought a lot of change. In addition to the adjustment of being married, we moved nearly two hours from my hometown of Fort Wayne. Chris and I knew we would be moving to the Indianapolis area when the trials were over. For so long, I couldn't wait to leave because I was tired of passing all the places in town that held terrible memories. But when the time actually came to settle into a new town, I found myself surprisingly stressed. Anytime I was stressed, the past would haunt me.

Trauma is an ever-shifting shadow. Even when the sun is shining, even after a fairy tale wedding, even when I am loved by a wonderful man, there is still an imprint on my soul that never fully disappears. Adjusting to a new city took me away from the triggers I had become used to experiencing but brought about a new set of triggers. I would have to learn to trust that I was safe in our new home; I would have to get comfortable with new routines, new neighbors, and life without the familiarity of my friends and family members living nearby.

Though our first year presented challenges of all kinds, I look back with nothing but gratitude. Despite all my doubts in the beginning and the twists and turns our stories have taken, the best decision of my life was becoming Mrs. Corrao.

Chapter Seventeen

A New Legacy

*Do things for people not because of who
they are or what they do in return, but because of
who you are.*
—Harold Kushner

While we were in Hawaii for our honeymoon, I began to feel a little off. I thought I had caught a virus after the busyness of the previous few months. But after we returned home, we were surprised to learn that I was expecting a baby just three months after we were married.

Chris and I had talked about having kids, and we were open to starting a family sooner than later. He was thirty-seven when we got married, and I was thirty-four, so we didn't feel like we had much time to waste. We hoped—

but weren't sure—that children would be in our future, so learning I was pregnant was a thrilling surprise.

On Chris's birthday, October 12, 1999, I gave birth to Christian Arthur Corrao. That was the only name that made sense. Christian as a namesake for the love of my life who shared his birthday and Arthur because, without Detective Arthur Billingsley, we would not be here nor would we have this miracle child.

When I first laid eyes on our him, I experienced a depth of love and gratitude I had never felt before. The first words that poured out of me when I saw him were, "Thank you, God, for this miracle!"

He was a gift of love straight from heaven. My body, which had once been treated like garbage and thrown away carelessly, had carried and delivered this perfect gift of grace. The feeling was indescribable.

While I was overjoyed about becoming a mom to Christian, life presented new challenges, and the old trauma still crept in. It was confusing. Why, when I was feeling so much joy, did uncomfortable feelings of sadness and anger still loom? I had everything I could ever want, so I felt guilty sharing how I felt with anyone. The strange relationship I had with life kept me tied to the trauma, even in the midst of positive circumstances, yet I didn't want the pain to overshadow the gratitude I felt for life, for love, and for all the good things in life.

In 2002, on the anniversary date of my attack, I learned that I lost a child. In November of that year, I made this journal entry:

A lot has happened, and I should have used this writing as a tool to my healing again. We found out I'd lost the baby I was pregnant with on September 12, 2002—two weeks after the news I had lost my job. Then we learned that Chris's salary was significantly reduced. No matter how many bad things that happen in your life, it does not mean you are not subject to more! I used to cry a lot or get more emotional over things. I don't cry much anymore. I don't know if that is good or bad. It's almost like I don't feel. I don't feel like I'm nice anymore. Maybe that is how I am dealing with it. It's a week until I start my new job . . . I feel lucky to have the chance to do what I have wanted to do. I hope it is a good change for Chris and me. We are struggling. I love him so much. My faith feels weak. I am using this time to let God have my burdens.

Within a year, I lost another baby. A specialist informed me that I had some physical issues that were keeping me from being able to carry a baby. When he learned that I had already carried Christian full-term and delivered without complications, he didn't have an explanation other than "miraculous."

The loss of two pregnancies, along with the doubts about whether I could ever have more children, caused stress and pain to surface. And, of course, pain triggered the trauma many times. I was lonely, grieving, and still trying to heal.

We were living almost two hours away from my therapist, Jocelyn, who had helped me so much, and I was feeling stuck. So I began to look for a way to continue healing in our new town. The local newspaper had a list of local resources, including a support group for victims of crime and abuse held by Prevail, a victim awareness and support program. I was grateful to find this resource and started attending once a week.

As I met and interacted with the other group members, I realized that most of them were trying to survive their trauma on their own. I had been blessed with such amazing help and therapy, and I soon realized that trauma survivors in the group were looking *to me* for support. The questions and struggles they brought to me helped me see how far I had come since the attack.

The facilitator, Deb, saw what was happening and invited me to become a co-facilitator for the group. Being able to help other people process their experiences began a major shift in my life. That shift ultimately led to the opportunity, for part-time work at Prevail, beginning in 2002.

On March 8, 2004, I gave birth to our beautiful and amazing daughter, Olivia Kristine Corrao. She gave me new eyes with which to see myself and the world around me. I was excited to have a daughter and a sibling for Christian, but having a girl came with another whole set of worries about how I would protect her from anything like what I had experienced.

Arthur Billingsley has become part of our family. Our kids have always known him as "Uncle Art." After Art and Leslie were married and eventually had kids, our families became increasingly closer. We still get together often to celebrate life throughout the year.

Every September 12th, I celebrate the gift of life by journaling and planning something fun to do. Each year since 1996, I have sent Art a "hero" gift and card and called him on the phone to hear his voice and thank him for saving my life. My body can sense when the anniversary date is approaching, and there are difficult emotions that come up around the date each year, but I use the occasion to choose gratitude for all that I've had the opportunity to experience. Because my life didn't end that day.

Over time, I have become acutely aware that the future I begged God for from the trunk of my car was not for me. God was not indulging me with a few more years of life merely for *my* benefit. My life was spared so I could leave a legacy that would follow me for generations.

I would come to understand that, regardless of the circumstances of my life or the pain I endured or the wrong done to me or the baffling injustices, none of it was *about* me. But it would require me showing up and being fully present for the sake of everyone whose lives mine would impact.

I had been so worried that my abduction would steal my identity, but the reality is, it only solidified it. I would discover strength I didn't know I had, not just in *spite* of my pain, but *because* of it.

I never want anyone to suffer what I suffered. It isn't fair or right. It steals so much. Facing tragedy has a way of stripping away everything we think we can't do without. But when we're still standing, even in the face of our worst nightmares, we realize we never needed all the things we held on to for safety.

The miracle of survival is the way a story we don't want can actually offer us the rare opportunity to see life from a vantage point we've never seen. And once we've seen that, we can no longer un-see it. We have new eyes with which to see others' suffering and a new understanding of what they need.

Those moments in my trunk, when I felt Jesus' compassionate presence crying with me, have given me a unique window into God's understanding of the battles we all face. I am increasingly convinced that He doesn't turn away from us in our lowest moments but, rather, settles in and weeps with us while we feel everything that pain brings into our lives. He knows firsthand how pain feels. Yet He doesn't leave us there. He gives us what we need so we can understand what others need. That's how our stories create a strong, beautiful tapestry of humanity that is interconnected with everyone who came before us and everyone who will follow.

Chris and I each endured many painful circumstances, yet we emerged stronger as individuals. That was the only way we could become stronger together. We would face many more difficult challenges in the years to come, but we knew we were part of something that would far outlast us. We were creating a new legacy.

Chapter Eighteen

What Prevails

*The things that go wrong for you have a lot of
potential to become part of your gift to the world.*
—Krista Tippett

ccording to the *Oxford English Dictionary*, the word *prevail* means "to prove more powerful than opposing forces; victorious." That definition describes what I learned as I began to work with people in crisis as a volunteer at Prevail. Working with victims of violent crime became a fulfilling way to prove that I was stronger than what happened to me. And I wanted to help others prevail, too.

When I first submitted my application and resume to the founder of Prevail, Beth Gehlhausen, she wondered why I, with my qualifications, would want a job as a receptionist. The answer was simple. I believed in the mission of the organization and wanted to be the first voice victims heard when they called Prevail for help.

During the interview process, I was introduced to Beth, as well as Susan Tibbs, both of whom would become comrades of mine during the next several years. I went on to serve the organization full-time as manager of community development and in five other positions, eventually becoming the assistant director.

I am still astounded by the opportunities I received there and the people I met. About five years after I joined the staff of Prevail, I told my story for the first time. We had started a monthly education series to offer the surrounding community an opportunity to learn about our support services. We wanted to share crucial information about the effects of crime and abuse on individuals, families, and communities.

At the encouragement of some of my coworkers, I decided to share my story at one of those monthly meetings. While I was nervous about what people would think of me and worried they might perceive me differently, I was also comforted by the fact that this meeting would only be attended by a small audience.

I expected that I would tell my story and check it off as something I needed to do; then I would move on with my life. However, in that audience was a woman named Judi Johnson, who approached me after the meeting and expressed how much other people needed to hear my story. She told me that, judging from my appearance, she would have never guessed what I had been through, and she spoke of how much hope I could bring to other victims of crime who needed to know they, too, could survive a similar story.

Her words took me back to the car ride home from the hospital when I was suddenly aware of the depth of pain people are going through in life and longed to connect with someone—anyone—who could understand what I had been through. I realized, for the first time in my life, that I had the opportunity to be that someone for other survivors.

Judi eventually joined the Prevail staff and not only encouraged me to tell my story but also created opportunities for me to do just that. She helped me create a speaker's bio, arranged for me to speak at local events, attended every speaking engagement, and even captured photos of me speaking to various audiences. Judi remains one of my greatest cheerleaders and has become one of my best friends.

I steadily moved into a public life of victim advocacy. The more I worked with survivors and began to understand first responders' roles, the more I became committed to helping improve victims' experiences. I worked closely with our county prosecutor to form a Sexual Assault Response Team (SART). This team ensures sexual assault victims get an effective, consistent, comprehensive, and collaborative response that prioritizes their needs and brings responsible persons to justice.

In the immediate aftermath of my attack, I didn't want to talk about it. But, over time, I discovered that telling my story not only helped other people believe there was hope for them but sharing my experiences brought me healing, too. For that reason, I began working with other survivors to provide support and opportunities when they were ready to tell their stories.

Through Prevail, I assembled a speaker's bureau for the purpose of empowering survivors to courageously share their experiences. These survivors now educate our community and provide a much-needed lifeline for other survivors, creating a ripple effect of healing and advocacy. Like me, these speakers have been amazed by what happens when good begins to flow out of the very experiences they once thought would be unredeemable.

What a privilege it was to go home every day knowing I was making a difference in someone's life. My work with Prevail opened up opportunities to share my story with first responders. That became life-giving work for me, to help first responders anticipate what people need in the most horrific moments of their lives. I was able to share with them how someone who has been traumatized feels and what is and is not helpful when the brain is in "fight or flight" mode.

My work with first responders opened the door for me to speak regularly at Sexual Assault Nurse Examiners' training courses offered at the Fort Wayne Sexual Assault Treatment Center where I was treated after the attack. In time, I was invited to participate in similar courses at the Center of Hope in Indianapolis.

Each time I shared my story, someone would come to me who needed a lifeline. And the more I shared my story, the more invitations I received. With each new opportunity, the size of the audience grew.

I was invited to Manchester College in Manchester, Indiana to speak about sexual assault on college campuses. Organizers of that event expected between sixty and eighty students to attend; however, more than three hundred came. And not only did they listen intently but many also stayed around for over an hour afterward to talk with me about their own experiences.

In 2007, the mayor of our city, Mayor Ditslear, invited me to share my story at The Mayor's Prayer Breakfast which I had attended in years past. I was honored by the invitation but was also aware that this event would be attended by peers and associates in my community who had no idea what my history entailed.

That day, looking out over the audience as I shared my story, I saw professionals from my community, including my priest, the fire chief, and numerous others whom I respected. Though I felt vulnerable at first, their support made me feel valued and helped me realize the power of telling my story.

Then something happened that caught me off-guard. I was nominated by the Indiana Criminal Justice Institute for an award called the Special Courage Award. This award is presented each year during National Crime

Victims' Rights week by the Attorney General and Office for Victims of Crime (OVC) at the U.S. Department of Justice.

I provided them with the information they requested, then didn't think much more about it. But a couple of months later, I received a call from Joy Frost, who was the acting director at OVC. She called to invite me to Washington, DC where I would receive the Special Courage Award.

The next thing I knew, Chris, Christian, Olivia, and I were on an airplane bound for Washington, DC. I was naive about the magnitude of that award and the opportunities it would present. Arthur Billingsley was recognized along with me, which was the most meaningful part of that experience. Twenty-five friends and family members showed up to offer their support. I truly felt that this opportunity and the incredible outpouring of support was not just for me but for all victims of crime and abuse.

Receiving an award for something that I didn't really do or ask for generated an unfamiliar mix of emotions. An event that had brought such pain was also giving me a platform from which I could provide hope for people who desperately needed a lifeline. I welcomed the opportunity unaware at the time of where this would lead.

At the National Crime Victims' Rights Week, I sat next to Judge Susan Carbon, who was the Director of the Office on Violence Against Women at the Justice Department, appointed by the President. She was moved by my story, and we connected right away. I later received a letter from Sue inviting me to join a panel of sixty experts in the field of sexual violence to meet at the White House and discuss ways sexual violence could be prevented on a national level.

As a result of receiving the Special Courage Award, Arthur and I were given the opportunity to speak at the National Sexual Response Team Conference, which was attended by more than one thousand first responders from all over the country. It was a surreal experience to be there, speaking with Art on a national platform, knowing how our lives first collided in those dark, life-altering moments years earlier.

I now know that whenever life appears to be nothing more than a series of mistakes and pain, you must keep going. It is not the end of the story. What prevails is hope.

I couldn't have possibly imagined where my story would take me, and it is still not over, but I finally understand that there are more good things in store for me, not in *spite* of my story but *because* of it.

Chapter Nineteen

It Doesn't Get Better than This

If I had my life to live over again, I would ask that not a thing be changed, but that my eyes be opened wider.

—Jules Renard

Chris and I have always been open with Christian and Olivia, especially about the story of my attack. As they've grown, both kids have become increasingly aware and involved in my work with victims of crime and abuse. I thank God every day for the family He gave me and how they have joined me in becoming a voice for people who desperately need to know someone understands their pain.

In October of 2016, one of those "it doesn't get any better than this" moments happened. Chris and I and both our kids were invited to speak at Fort Riley, a US Army base near Manhattan, Kansas, where we shared not just my story but *our* story.

I met SFC Bethany Guzman when I spoke at the National Sexual Assault Conference a year earlier, and she expressed at the time how adamant she was about getting me to her army base to speak. Knowing how survivors' families are affected by sexual assault, she invited our entire family to speak to the families living at Fort Riley.

We would speak to four thousand soldiers and family members over the course of two days as part of their Sexual Assault Awareness Response & Prevention Program, each from our own perspective. When we weren't speaking, we were treated like royalty. We enjoyed a full schedule of exciting activities and had an amazing time learning about life on an army base.

The highlight of the weekend—honestly, a highlight of my life—happened when we started speaking. Anytime I tell my story, something special happens; it just feels right. But this time, after I spoke, I watched in awe as Chris passionately shared the raw realities that came with watching me suffer in the aftermath of the trauma. He had never spoken of our story publicly, yet he poured out his heart, explaining how his love for me kept him going. In his voice was a tenderness and compassion for anyone who had faced a similar situation.

The audience was invited to ask questions, and our kids had agreed in advance to answer questions directed to them. But there was no way I could prepare for what they would say. I was blown away to hear them verbalize, for the first time, how my story had impacted them.

Christian was sixteen years old at the time and spoke from his heart like a pro. When asked how the kids found out, he made the audience laugh when he shared about the day he asked me if Uncle Art was really his uncle. "Can't you see the resemblance?" he said with a smile as their picture was shown on the screen behind us. His humor broke the heaviness in the room at just the perfect moment.

Without even realizing it, Olivia answered the last question more beautifully than we could have possibly planned. She said, through tears, that as strange as it may sound, her mom wouldn't be the person she is if the attack hadn't happened and that she wouldn't want me to be any different.

I almost couldn't breathe as I listened to my husband and our two kids share with such grace this story that had started with so much pain. This was the family I'd always hoped for, the story I never imagined.

For so long after my assault, I wanted to avoid the grief that seemed to engulf me. I tried to go over it, around it, and under it, only to find that the only path toward healing was to go through it. If I hadn't allowed myself to fully experience the grief—even when I was convinced I'd taken a thousand steps backward—I couldn't have stood there alongside my family to experience this redemptive moment.

Flashing through my mind, as if on a movie screen were the faces of the amazing people who had made it possible for me to stand tall beside my family on that day—people I'd met because of the most horrific experience of my life. I felt immense gratitude for the founder of Prevail, Beth Gehlhausen, who had the vision to create a place where victims' voices can be heard, where they are believed, and where they can receive support. I realized how sharing my story to one small group of people had introduced me to Judi and opened up a whole new realm of possibilities for me to help other women find their way forward and, perhaps someday, tell their own stories.

I was reminded that Karen Hensel, one of the anchor women who gravely reported my abduction on the evening news so many years ago, had become a voice of advocacy as the emcee for Prevail's annual fundraising gala. When I first shared with her that I was the victim in that news story, we began engaging in important conversations about how the media reports on crime and how to ensure that respect for victims does not get lost in the quest for higher ratings.

I remembered the friendship that developed with Susan Carbon after we served on the panel together at the White House, and I felt hopeful that our shared passion for ending sexual violence could truly make a difference. I couldn't believe how the ripple effects of sharing my story one time, for a handful of people, had led to so many incredible experiences for me and, now, for my family.

I used to think sharing such a personal story might make others uncomfortable with me, but I was so wrong. After we spoke at Fort Riley, we were overwhelmed by the comments we received. One soldier wrote, "Sitting in the audience and looking at pictures from the crime scene and watching the local news cover the story was heartbreaking. Listening to Michelle tell her story and what she needed at the time for support . . . Everyone should hear."

Another wrote, "Christian and Olivia have no fear! They are the most mature kids at their age that I have ever seen . . . I learned a lot from those two kids telling their stories, and I am twenty years older than them!"

"Chris Corrao did amazing telling his side of the story and how it affected him," someone else commented. "He sends a strong message, and to hear him speak for the first time made me shed so many tears. Michelle and Chris have a strong message to tell . . . They are truly special."

"I have never been so moved by a guest speaker before," another soldier shared. "To actually hear a spouse's side of the story—what he went through to support her—is what everyone needs to hear . . . Sexual violence happens every day, but people do not realize the impact it has not only to the victim but to the family as well. Being able to ask the entire family questions in person and to see where they are today was incredible."

These comments, and too many others to share here, poured in. Pages and pages of feedback confirmed to us that we were on the right path. The combination of education about sexual violence and our personal experiences resonated with people in a way I couldn't have possibly predicted. Hearing the words of those who had been so deeply affected by our story helped us understand, as never before, that we were able to help soothe others' pain because of our own.

That experience at Fort Riley was the culmination of years of healing. I couldn't have possibly imagined the events of that weekend during the early days following my sexual assault. It is so important to understand that when a person is overwhelmed with the pain of trauma, worrying about all the weeks, months, and years to come is not helpful. The only way forward was to take one moment at a time and simply keep breathing, keep saying yes to life.

Often, after I tell my story, I am asked the question, "If you could go back and change anything, knowing how your life would turn out, would you?"

Now, I can honestly answer that question with a resounding no.

I wouldn't change a moment of the pain in order to experience the depths of love from my family or the life-altering friendships that have come into my life. I wouldn't wish an attack like that on anyone, yet it taught me that I can trust my gut and that I am far more resilient than I ever knew. It taught me to learn how to ask for help, then to give help to others in return. It taught me to be grateful for every good day, every breath, and every person who crosses my path.

There is a sign hanging in our bathroom that perfectly sums up what I have come to believe as a survivor: "Life doesn't get any better than this." I see it first thing every morning as a reminder. The same sign hangs on the wall by our back door to read every time we leave our home.

It's really true. We have *right now,* and that's all we we're meant to handle at one time. Trusting the process of healing, of love, of faith, and of life really boils down to learning to appreciate each moment for the possibility it holds to arm us with exactly what we need.

The past matters, but we aren't there now. And the future will matter, but we're not there yet. It has become extremely important to me not to get caught up in what happened in yesterday's battles or in my hopes and dreams for the future but to rest in the infinite gift of this moment I'm living in right now.

Life is far from perfect, but somehow Love has a way of seeking us out in our darkest moments. And just when we think all is lost, to our amazement, we are found.

About the Authors

Michelle Corrao

Michelle Corrao is a keynote speaker and compassionate advocate for victims of violent crime. For eighteen years she served at Prevail, a victim awareness and support program, where she led the charge to create Central Indiana's Sexual Assault Response Team (SART), focused on victim-centered, trauma-informed care.

She is the recipient of the Special Courage Award, presented by the US Attorney General (2010), and became first-ever recipient of the Distinguished Hoosier Award, presented by the Indiana Attorney General.

Through Michelle's current role as executive director at The O'Connor House in Carmel, Indiana, she leads programs that provide women who are single, pregnant, and homeless with safe housing and opportunities to improve life for themselves and their children.

Michelle speaks to audiences of influencers, first responders, medical professionals, military and law enforcement personnel, faith communities, and a broad scope of conferences and events aimed at creating stronger, safer communities.

Need a speaker for your event?

Please visit Michelle's website at www.michellecorrao. com or contact me at michellecorrao@gmail.com

Do you have an outreach...

to jails, prisons, juvenile centers, women's shelters, or other crisis intervention groups? Please consider using this book as a reference for how God can change their lives.

Emily Sutherland

Emily Sutherland is an internationally recognized storyteller whose body of work spans a broad spectrum of genres and mediums, including scriptwriting for television and radio, authoring and co-authoring books, ghostwriting, songwriting, magazine features, photojournalism, podcasts, and blogging.

With more than twenty years as an executive staff member in the music industry, her name appears in the credits of dozens of *Billboard* chart-topping volumes produced by Gaither Television Productions and Coming Home Music Productions. Her multifaceted roles have provided opportunities to excel in a variety of disciplines, including mass communications, photojournalism, artist management, video production, web content creation, public relations, and on-camera interviews.

Her unique specialty is finding the heart and soul inside every story with a blend of raw authenticity and genuine compassion. She has lent her voice to countless biographical stories and published works on the subjects of creativity, spirituality, relationships, leadership, hospitality, and personal growth.

Emily also serves as a mentor and coach to help others write their stories. She launched her one-day Storytelling School in 2020 to teach others the tools and processes she uses to write stories and manuscripts.

Emily and her husband, Scott, are cofounders of the Love Better movement and hosts of The Love Better Podcast (www.lovebetter.world). Through storytelling and gatherings, they lead conversations on how individuals' daily choices can contribute to making the world a more loving place.

You are invited to learn more about Emily's work and connect with her online at: emilysutherland.me.

Resources

Office of Victims of Crime (OVC)
www.OVC.gov
800-851-3420

www.remedylive.com
24/7 Online Chat Center
Text REMEDY to 494949 to chat about abuse, anxiety, bullying, depression, drugs and alcohol, eating disorders, faith, pornography,self-harm, suicide

Suicide Prevention
Call 1-800-273-TALK (8255)

Crisis Text Line
Text HOME to 741741
www.crisistextline.org

PAVE (Promoting Awareness I Victim Empowerment)
PAVE is a movement creating a world free from sexual
violence and building communities to support survivors.
www.shatteringthesilence.org.

Sex Trafficking
Are you being forced to do anything you do not want to do?
Have you been threatened if you   try to leave? Have you
witnessed young girls being prostituted? If so, please call the
National Human Trafficking Hotline (24/7) at 1-888-373-7888.